The
Restorer's Handbook
of
Furniture

Under the direction of Madeleine Hours, chief curator of the National Museums of France, Master of Research at the National Center for Scientific Research.

The
Restorer's Handbook
of
Furniture

Daniel Alcouffe

 VAN NOSTRAND REINHOLD COMPANY

New York Cincinnati Toronto London Melbourne

English translation: J. A. Underwood

Copyright © 1977 by Office du Livre, Fribourg (Switzerland)

Library of Congress Catalog Card Number: 77-5589

ISBN 0-442-20281-4

Printed in Switzerland

Published in 1977 by Van Nostrand Reinhold Company
A division of Litton Educational Publishing, Inc.
450 West 33rd Street, New York, NY 10001, U.S.A.

Van Nostrand Reinhold Limited
1410 Birchmount Road, Scarborough, Ontario MIP 2 E 7, Canada

Van Nostrand Reinhold Australia Pty. Ltd.
17 Queen Street, Mitcham, Victoria 3132, Australia

Van Nostrand Reinhold Company Limited
Molly Millars Lane, Wokingham, Berkshire, England

16 15 14 13 12 11 10 9 8 7 6 5 4 3 2 1

Library of Congress Cataloging in Publication Data

Alcouffe, Daniel.

The restorer's handbook of furniture.

Translation of Restauration du mobilier.

Bibliography: p. 126

Includes index.

1. Furniture – Repairing.
I. Title.

TT 199.A 5213   684.1'044   77-5589

ISBN 0-442-20281-4

TABLE OF CONTENTS

INTRODUCTION 7

MATERIALS AND TOOLS 19
Materials 19
    Wood 19
    Glue 21
    Modern adhesives 24
Tools 25

TYPES OF DAMAGE 27
Causes 27
Rot and worm damage 30
    Disinfection 31
    Consolidation 32
    Prevention 33

WOODWORK 34
Stripping gilding and paintwork 34
    Dry stripping 34
    Chemical stripping 34
    Hot-water stripping 34
    Potassium stripping 35

Dismantling 36
Distortion 37
Filling 37
Filling dents 38
Repairing tenons 38
Splits 38
Consolidating joints and gluings 40
    Joints in the thickness of the wood 40
    Inlays 42
    Strengthening pieces used inside 42
New pieces 47
    Scarf gluing 47
    False rebate 48
    Carving 48
Drawer slides 48

VENEER 49
Ungluing veneer 52
Replacements 55
Regluing veneer 60
    Regluing with a veneering hammer 60
    Caul veneering 61
        Cauls 62
        Pressing 64

Strap veneering 65
Tarsia certosina 66

FINISHING VARNISHED AND WAXED FURNITURE 67

Stripping 67
Rubbing down 67
Staining 69
Varnishing, wax filling, wax polishing 71
  French polishing 74
    Filling 74
    Varnishing 75
    Polishing 76
    Reviving varnish 78
Wax filling 78
Wax polishing 80

BOULLE MARQUETRY 81

Removing all the marquetry 84
  Ungluing 84
  Replacing missing pieces 86
  Levelling off 89
  Regluing 90
  Finishing 90

GILDING AND PAINTWORK 93

Gilding 93
  Water gilding 93
    Restoring the woodwork 97
    Cleaning 97
    Refixing flakes 97
    Patching 97
    Complete renewal of gilding 98

    Degreasing 98
    Sizing 100
    Ground 100
    Trimming 102
    Ochre sizing 102
    The bed 102
    Gilding 104
    Burnishing 106
    Matting 106
    Patina 106
  Oil gilding 109
  Silvering 110
Paintwork 110

AUXILIARY TECHNIQUES 111

Upholstery 111
Bronze mounts 112
  Soldering 112
  Cleaning 113
Marble 113

CARE AND MAINTENANCE 114

NOTES AND DIAGRAMS 116

BIBLIOGRAPHY 126

ACKNOWLEDGEMENTS 127

INDEX 128

INTRODUCTION

Where the history of a piece of furniture can be traced from documentary evidence, it reads like a chapter of accidents; where, as is usually the case, its history is unknown, one has every ground for suspecting the worst. There is hardly a piece of antique furniture in existence today that has not at some stage in its career undergone repair.[1] And as far as conserving the piece in its original state is concerned, until recently such repairs were more often than not prejudicial.

Furniture restoration is indeed no new phenomenon. The evidence shows that from the time when furniture started to become more sophisticated and more decorative it was maintained and repaired for as long as the particular piece concerned remained in fashion. For the seventeenth and eighteenth centuries our sources are the account books of the wealthy and the records of manufacturers.[2] Big houses sometimes employed staff specifically for this purpose. Or the manufacturer might offer a maintenance service: in 1702 Sigismond Flexan, a cabinet-maker of the Faubourg Saint-Antoine, Paris, is recorded as having sold a customer a bureau 'which he undertakes to repair for him in the event of its showing any fault of workmanship'.[3] Later, under Louis XV, the day-book of the Parisian dealer Duvaux mentions various restoration jobs: 'To repairing two commodes, re-veneering and renovating them; also refurbishing the mounts...' (1749); 'To repairing two lacquered commodes; restoring the carcase and drawers, rubbing down the old aventurine varnish, renewed in black by Martin, restoring the lacquer and adding reliefs to mask faults, redipping and renewing the mounts, 175 l.' (1752); 'To repairing, rubbing down and renovating a commode; redipping the mounts in powdered gold paint, 48 l.' (1755).[4] But the tendency in this period was for a piece of furniture, no matter what its quality, to be regarded not as a work of art but as a utilitarian or purely decorative object requiring no special care. It was restored in order to keep it looking new at all cost, not with a view to posterity. Riesener, restoring a piece for Louis XV, 'scrapes and repolishes' the marquetry and cleans the gilding on the mounts as often as he is asked to.[5] And when a piece became obsolete people had no hesitation in making it larger or higher or changing the veneer or the mounts, as Pierre Verlet's researches into the furniture of the French royal family have shown. If adaptation was impossible, the piece was abandoned. Louis XIV, for example, possessed virtually no furniture that had belonged to his predecessors. It was the tradition of the 'Garde-Meuble de la Couronne', the Crown Furniture Repository, 'to hold from time to time a sale of old furniture no longer in service'.[6] A practice recorded as early as the eighteenth century was that of re-using on new furniture elements from old pieces that had been broken up, whether Boulle marquetry panels,[7] hard-stone mosaic work,[8] or late sixteenth-century architectural inlaid work from Germany.[9]

With the advent of the nineteenth century there was a change. Contemporary furniture continued to be overhauled in the same way,[10] but a number of craftsmen began to specialize in the restoration of antique furniture. Their names were circulated in such publications as the Paris *Almanach du Commerce*. We know for example that in the reign of Louis XVIII one Smith 'makes and also restores every kind of antique painted furniture' and that between 1836 and 1844 the inlayer Brunet undertook 'the repair of precious items of furniture'.[11]

The fashion for and commercial exploitation of antique furniture were in fact beginning to emerge. Antique furniture was appreciated but still not respected. Its restoration was directed not at preserving the piece but at turning what was left of it to the best possible advantage from both the utilitarian and the aesthetic points of view. At first ingenuously but subsequently with a view to profit, restorers would take a piece of antique furniture and either reconstitute it according to what they believed to have been its original appearance or alter it to meet contemporary needs. Often keeping those elements still in good condition, they would complete the piece by means of fragments taken from other antique pieces. Under Louis XVIII the *Bazar parisien* wrote of the cabinet-maker Rémond that 'he also makes furniture using old Chinese lacquer-work, restores furniture, and makes up pieces according to the tastes of those who come to him'.[12]

This approach is recorded even among the most gifted connoisseurs. At first it was medieval and Renaissance furniture that attracted attention, and one of the earliest French collectors was the painter Revoil, among whose finest pieces was a sixteenth-century wardrobe, sold to the Louvre in 1828 along with the rest of his collection: 'When M. Revoil acquired the piece the pediment was missing. Unable to leave such a masterpiece incomplete, the antiquarian made one up himself, seeing fit to introduce the H's and the crescents (Henri II and Diane de Poitiers)'[13] – and so falsifying the appearance, decoration and history of the piece. Louis-Philippe purchased for the Château de Pau some late medieval and Renaissance furniture of which at the end of the century this was said: 'Credences and chests became – to meet the requirements of modern living – cabinets and commodes. We acknowledge readily, nevertheless, that as a rule repairs were carried out with adequate regard if not for the original forms at least for the carving and general decoration.'[14]

Subsequently seventeenth-century furniture came to be altered in the same way. In ordering a 'Boulle-style piece' from Jacob Desmalter fils in 1834 the Crown Furniture Repository supplied him with antique panels of brass and tortoise-shell inlaid work.[15] Mid-seventeenth-century French ebony cabinets were, depending on their condition, broken up or adapted as bases for two-piece wardrobes. This was one of the specialities of Edward Holmes Baldock, a London dealer who in 1843 was selling doors and panels taken from this type of piece.[16] When from the Second Empire onwards it was the turn of eighteenth-century furniture to be collected, it too sometimes received scant respect, notwithstanding the importance of the period as far as the evolution of the decorative arts is concerned. Wood was stripped down, mounts changed – in fact things got so bad that in 1908 the collector Paul Eudel protested: 'The exception proving the rule, it can be stated as a general principle that there is no such thing as a piece of antique furniture any more. Everything sold is either a fake or has been hideously repaired. Of the secular furniture of bygone eras virtually nothing has survived.'[17]

But it is in our own day that, in living conditions for which it was not designed, such antique furniture as is still around has undergone the most rapid deterioration. Our job is to rescue what we can. In fact furniture restoration is becoming something of a priority business – and one on which increasing demands are being made as collectors become better informed and more anxious to preserve their inheritance and as, with the supply running dry, badly damaged pieces are coming on the market that no one would have thought of restoring before.

One regrettable feature of this situation is that some collectors decide for reasons of economy to do their own restoring. When the 'do-it-yourself' columns tell you that restoration is easy, take them with a pinch of salt. What happens is that the amateur starts a job fairly successfully, is emboldened to continue, and sooner or later perpetrates a disaster that means the end of a work that could have been saved. Do-it-yourself restoration almost invariably does more harm than good; restoration is a job for the professional, a delicate and difficult job that places grave responsibilities on the shoulders of anyone undertaking it and is further complicated nowadays by the dearth of qualified practitioners, suitable materials and equipment.

Once upon a time – say, fifty years ago – restoration

was easy because the public was relatively undemanding. Manufacturers were doing well and attracted the good men, while the not-so-good cabinet-makers set up as restorers. Nowadays the public is more discerning and expects restorers to be top-flight craftsmen. The question is whether top-flight craftsmen are going to be available in future. A combination of circumstances – the present fad for handicrafts, the economic depression, which means that manufacturers are laying off staff, and the possibility of setting up on one's own early in life – have led to a spate of somewhat impromptu vocations. Furniture restoring, however, calls for special training in view of the number and variety of the skills its practitioners must have literally at their finger-tips.

The first necessity is a deep knowledge of antique furniture, acquired primarily through observation in museums and through studying the specialist literature. One of the reasons why such disastrous mistakes were made in the past was ignorance; blindly following preconceived ideas in the absence of any culture of his own, the restorer might decide that such and such a modification was necessary or that such and such an element must be removed as unoriginal – and be totally wrong.

Then, on the technical level, restoration calls for more skills than manufacture. The furniture restorer must be a craftsman of wide and varied experience – as varied, in fact, as the tasks he will be confronted with. He must be able to do everything: assembly, carving, marquetry, incised work, japanning, and so on. It is desirable that anyone going in for restoration should combine a technical, academic education with a period of practical training in a restoration studio, whereby the academic side must be all the more thorough for the fact that certain techniques, which are in the process of dying out, cannot be handed down in an adulterated form. Ideally would-be restorers, on leaving college, would spend some time with a manufacturer before specializing in the restoration branch. Here, however, we come across another problem, which is that one is asking a lot of an established restorer to spend much of his time instructing others. Many craftsmen wish sincerely to pass on their skills, but this is not made easy for them. It is not enough for a recruit to spend a short time in a well-known studio in order to obtain a reference before setting up on his own; a restorer only starts to become useful after several years' training.

Another problem facing restorers today is the difficulty of setting up a business in the centres of big cities, which means that they are always at a distance from their clientele.[18] On the other hand finding a clientele is no problem, given the widespread interest in antique furniture. The restorer will need to educate it, however, explaining to the collector that restoring a piece of furniture is a long and costly business. The time factor is not really surprising, because anything may happen during the course of a job to hold it up: for example a piece of veneer that looks all right initially may turn out on closer examination to be completely faked, covered with pieces, perforated, etc. The cost of restoration is due not to the materials used – these hardly ever add up to very much – but to the labour; what makes it expensive is all the work of which there is afterwards no sign on the surface of the piece: consolidating the carcase of veneered furniture, preparing the ground for gilding, and so on. One must make it clear to people that spending money on res-

toration is in the nature of a long-term investment. It is good policy in this respect to invite the customer into the studio before starting on his job, show him pieces of furniture undergoing restoration, and have him back at various stages of the job to keep him informed and see what he thinks.

If the amount of work involved is the same, a simple piece of furniture will cost as much to restore as an elaborate piece, so where does one draw the line? Should one quietly abandon pieces of minor interest that would cost too much to restore? The answer of course is no: it is better in a case like this to adopt a temporary solution, doing merely what is most urgent.

It is a good idea for the restorer to take a few precautions. One of these will be to photograph each piece of furniture before he sets about restoring it. And if he has any doubts about its authenticity he had better communicate them to the owner at the outset, even at the risk of annoying him by implicitly questioning his competence. Otherwise, if the piece does later turn out to be a fake, the restorer may be accused of having substituted a copy or of having involved the owner in needless expense.

Unfortunately the sheer cost of a day's labour, coupled sometimes with the fact of insurance deadlines, often forces good restorers to work faster than they would like, setting a limit to the time they can spend on each piece of furniture. Yet it is vital that, before he does anything else, the restorer should have time to think, time to pass under review the various treatments possible in each particular case. Restoration, as we have already suggested, is more difficult than manufacture. The manufacturer follows certain rules, but restoration cannot be codified. The solution will depend on a number of factors: the state of the wood, the period of the piece, its shape, structure, decoration, and so on. It will also depend on where the piece is to go; a chair that is going to be subjected to everyday use will need to be more solidly repaired than a chair that is going to be roped off in the stable atmosphere of a museum. Every piece of furniture is a case apart. Moreover restoring a piece of furniture does not mean going all out to recreate a presumed original state; it means above all halting the process of decay and consolidating what is left in such a way as not to impair its appearance.

As far as possible the restorer should obtain this result by using the same methods, tools and materials as the man who made the piece in the first place. The proof of these traditional methods is in the fact that the piece has already lasted for so long. Nevertheless one must not be dogmatic. The piece is to be preserved by any and every means available – including, occasionally, compromise solutions. Some restorers, out of respect for the work they are treating, will be reluctant to employ a particular process because it was not in use 'then' and so is technically unorthodox. In extreme cases, however, it seems to me preferable for example to strengthen a flimsy piece with metal brackets and screws rather than enter the risk of dismantling it, or to patch up a piece of veneer rather than remove it and risk not being able to complete it correctly. Restoration is very much a creative job; the restorer is always having to invent solutions to make his repairs more effective while at the same time keeping them invisible – not with any fraudulent intent but in order not to diminish the work aesthetically.

Granted these reservations, it is still possible to lay down certain principles that ought to be respected:

Conserve a maximum of original material

This should be obvious: as much as possible of the old piece must be preserved and as little as possible added. Rather than renew original material it is better, in difficult cases, to effect a repair that can be seen or will show up eventually. Wood should be replaced only if it is intolerably worm-eaten, in the case of a solid element, or perforated, in the case of veneer.

Avoid radical measures

Some restorers see their task as being to carry out a complete overhaul. Systematically they dismantle the piece, remove the veneer, and strip off gilding and paintwork. This makes repairs simpler, and it is of course easier to draw up an estimate if one knows in advance that one is going to do everything. But this is renovating, not restoring, and such measures should be resorted to only when absolutely necessary. They may rob the piece of something of its antique character, and there is always the danger that one may break a joint or reassemble the piece out of true.

Another convenient but unacceptable solution is to eliminate any original elements one is unable to restore. For example in the absence of the right kind of wood to repair a piece of veneer, instead of using a similar wood the restorer may replace the whole panel with another that he has available. Or if one of a set of identical mounts is missing and he is unable to make a new one, the restorer may prefer to remove the whole lot. Similarly, other cabinet-makers retouch the old patina to make it match the new pieces they have added, which is easier than doing the job the other way round.

Respect the effects of ageing

Often the original colour of a piece of furniture will have been very bright, as can be seen sometimes on the inside or underneath the mounts. Even where external protection has been provided, air and light will inevitably have aged the surface of the wood. Trying to rub down to the original colour is out of the question; the risk would be too great, particularly in the case of veneered furniture. Natural ageing should be respected as part of the life and history of the piece. Moreover if the wood is made to look too new it will no longer harmonize with the other elements – mounts, upholstery, etc. – which will also have aged.

Do *not* dogmatically remove old repairs and alterations

Some restorers think that all old repairs should be redone on the grounds that they are visible or of unorthodox execution. In fact it is often better to retain them if they are still good, particularly in less visible places, rather than take the risks involved in removing them at all costs. In the old days restorers sometimes made the mistake of repairing with nails, which are often difficult to extract; persistent attempts to do so may make a hole and damage the piece further.

Similarly, faced with a piece of furniture that appears to have been altered, restorers are often tempted to re-establish what must have been or what they imagine must have been the original state of the piece, reconstituting what has been removed or taking away what appears to have been added. Firstly, one must be very sure in one's mind that one is in fact dealing with alterations. Secondly, changes of both form and decoration are sometimes themselves of great antiquity. The history of famous pieces of furniture offers many examples of alterations that were carried out at a very early stage.[19] Duvaux's day-book records modifications carried out on contemporary furniture: 'To de-veneering the pedestals of a writing-table, changing the drawers, and making two at the sides' (1750); 'To cutting down a bookcase of violet wood… re-veneering it in the same wood… recutting the marble and elaborating the mouldings' (1756).[20] There are also examples of ornamentation being altered for political reasons: in 1795 a Parisian cabinet-maker by the name of Périn restored a Boulle wardrobe on which he substituted 'various ornamental portions for others representing figures characteristic of the feudal system'.[21] Where mounts appear to have been added, this too may have been done early on, as we learn again from Duvaux's day-book: 'One powder-gilt clasp added to a marquetry leg' (1756); 'A Boulle commode… decorated all over with powder-gilt bronze, 600 l. Extending two masks on the sides, 60 l.' (1758).[22] Alterations of this kind may constitute evidence of the tastes or history of a particular period or individual. By removing them the restorer will have suppressed the whole history of the piece without even being sure that he has recaptured its original state.

A piece of restoration need not be made invisible at all cost

Many excellent restorers, believing this to be the key criterion of their work, make it a point of honour to conceal all trace of it. Persuaded by some of their clients, they consider that visible restorations throw suspicion on a piece of furniture and lower its value. For this reason they sometimes go to costly and unnecessary lengths to cover up their interventions, for example cutting blocks from old wood in order to pass them off as old repairs, or scoring the backs of new pieces of veneer with toolmarks designed to make them look hand-sawn.

At the other extreme archaeological restoration, in which the restored portions are deliberately left visible as such, is out of the question as far as furniture is concerned. Here any restorations must blend in with the rest of the piece; even if they are visible close to, from a distance they must leave the work harmonious and legible as a whole. This is achieved by the often difficult process of retouching the restored portions to match those that have not been treated.

One inexcusable practice is deliberately to inflict damage on replacement material in order to make it look like the rest of the piece, imitating worm-holes, blemishes and stains on gilding or paintwork. It is better to leave the new piece undamaged, even at the risk of having it look slightly awkward.

Only complete missing elements on the basis of unimpeachable information

What does one do when part of the structure or decoration of a piece of furniture is missing (ills. 1–4)? The problem arises for example when the stretcher of a chair has been removed, leaving only the plugged mortices in the legs, or when a piece of marquetry has been partially worn away. The restorer ought not to attempt to reconstitute unless he has an identical or symmetrical element that he can take as a model. This element may be on the piece itself, on a similar piece belonging to the same set – in the case of chairs, for example – or, pieces of furniture having been frequently repeated, on another example where one is known. Where decoration – carving, incised work, gilding, mounts – has disappeared or needs to be redone on a new piece, the restorer takes a tracing or plaster-cast of the model, as the case may be, and reproduces it strictly in the spirit of the original.

Where the problem becomes much trickier is where the missing element was the only one on the piece and no other example is known. Restorers have often gone wrong here. Where the missing portion is essential to the balance of the piece or where this makes no sense without it, the restorer may have no alternative but to reconstitute. Clearly if a piece designed to take a marble top has lost that top, it must be replaced. Here an old description of the piece may sometimes provide information about the missing portion, its dimensions, material, and so on. Some restorers draw on pieces of antique furniture they have known or use actual models taken from pieces they have restored in the past, but this is always a bit of a gamble; evidence may subsequently turn up to show that the reconstituted element is all wrong. The best advice to restorers here is: never invent, and always photograph the piece before you do anything.

It is preferable not to reconstitute in the absence of a reliable model. Granted, the piece will no longer present its original appearance, but at best one might not have recaptured this exactly, and at worst one might have got even farther away from it. Particularly as far as decoration is concerned it is important not to pervert the spirit of the piece by adding elements that might subsequently be taken for original. Nor should one try to disguise lacunae of any size; marks where mounts are missing should for example be left visible.

14

1

A seventeenth-century Boulle marquetry cabinet converted by the addition of a marble top, a base and four legs (1.15 m high, 0.95 m wide, and 0.44 m deep). We know of several similar cabinets that suffered the same fate in the late eighteenth and the nineteenth centuries.

2

The original base of the cabinet in ill. 1, converted at the same time into a console table by the addition of a marble top (1.15 m by 1 m by 0.50 m).

3

The cabinet and base of ills. 1 and 2 reassembled, all the added elements having been removed (1.85 m by 0.99 m by 0.50 m). The job was done at the end of the last century by Emile Molinier, curator at the Louvre, who used old descriptions of the piece, a seventeenth-century drawing of a similar piece, and the example of other pieces in a better state of preservation (Paris, Louvre Museum).

4

Antoine-Robert Gaudreaus: pair of violet wood prayer stools, Paris, *c.* 1745 (0.81 m by 0.61 m). The kneeler on the right-hand one, which had been removed, was restored in 1976 on the model of the one on the left (Fontainebleau, Musée national du Château).

Never try to 'improve' a piece of antique furniture

To some people restoration still means something more like transformation. It is a case either of the skilled restorer giving his creative imagination too much rope, or of his being encouraged to do so by dealers with whose heresies he is for economic reasons obliged to comply and for whom the increment value of the modified piece covers the cost of 'restoring' it. They leave the well-known pieces alone, but a lot can be done with an unknown piece

15

in the way of passing off a hack as a thoroughbred. Treating the piece of furniture as his raw material, the transformer-restorer sets about making it more harmonious, more practical and more attractive. Anything that is no longer in fashion is suppressed. On the assumption that the man who made the piece originally did not know what he was doing, alleged defects are removed, proportions are altered where they appear to be wrong or unusual (regardless of the fact that the piece may have been made like that to order), or for example the apron of a commode is changed to give it a more agreeable outline, the curve of the legs is modified, fluting is added, allegedly unaesthetic mounts or marquetry are replaced, and a piece is gilded that was originally plain. Often acting in good faith, the skilful restorer with an unscrupulous customer may soon become in effect a forger. Nineteenth-century restorers so thoroughly perverted the furniture of the Middle Ages and the Renaissance that it has become difficult to study and form an opinion about it. We

5
A letter-head stuck on a Louis XVI secretaire, underneath the marble.

must not let the same mistake be repeated on the furniture of later periods. Antique furniture has suffered enough; let us leave it as it has come down to us and not mutilate it further.

Carefully preserve all information figuring on the piece
Labels, marks, numbers written on the webbing — these all offer possibilities of retracing the history of the piece. If an element bearing such clues has to be replaced, the information should be transferred to the new portion.
The present work does not pretend to cover all the techniques and materials used and cases encountered in the restoration of antique furniture. Oriental and European lacquer-work in particular, which merit a study of their own, are not dealt with.

16

The problems and solutions are, as I have said, different in each case. It is no part of my intention to teach good restorers their job, except possibly to advise certain of them to adopt a more cautious approach. My purpose is rather to make clear to collectors or curators of antique furniture that the long and difficult task of restoring a piece of furniture is not one to be embarked upon lightly. Often a collector will hand a piece over to a restorer in good faith and not give it another thought until he receives it back – apparently in good condition. But what has happened to it meanwhile? Terrible things, sometimes, and it is important that collectors should have the courage – born of knowledge – to reject the suggestions some restorers will put to them.

One final word. The restoration of a piece of furniture can sometimes reveal a great deal about the way in which it was made, who made it, and what has happened to it since. That restoration completed, it is an excellent idea to leave somewhere inside the piece a record of who restored it and when, together with any pertinent observations[23] (ill. 5).

6

David Roentgen: secretaire, Neuwied, 1779 (3.69 m by 1.52 m by 0.88 m). The door of the upper part, with its pictures of astronomers, was missing. Roentgen made another, similar piece in the same year, and what is more he decorated it with the same marquetry panels (Berlin, Kunstgewerbe Museum), so the door of that piece was taken as a model when this piece was restored in 1953. Using a coloured photograph that gave him the kinds of wood and their colours, the restorer blew it up, traced it on to a mount, and reproduced the marquetry work exactly (Vienna, Oesterreichisches Museum für angewandte Kunst).

MATERIALS AND TOOLS

Materials

Furniture restorers in every field complain that the traditional materials they need for their work no longer have the properties they once had and have in many cases become difficult to obtain through lack of demand. Some have even completely disappeared, which has meant that certain traditional processes have been abandoned. Restorers are obliged to build up stocks by buying those of workshops that go out of business.[1]

7
Indigenous timbers (i.e. to France). Left to right and top to bottom: oak, beech, walnut, wild cherry, pear, bird's-eye maple, ash, plane, olive, box, sycamore, plum (with the sap-wood on the left), and green-dyed pear (the last three being represented by samples of saw-cut veneer with the upper part rubbed down; see also ill. 8).

8
Exotic veneers. Left to right and top to bottom:
1. Sawn with the grain: rosewood, violet wood, king wood, Brazilian rosewood, Cuban mahogany, ebony and snakewood. The saw has left regular marks that are still visible on the bottom part of these samples, the top part having been rubbed down.
2. Sawn across the grain: violet wood.
3. Sliced: thuya burr, amboyna, citrus.

In spite of these difficulties, however, there is no acceptable alternative to using those materials, even if they are no longer in peak condition. As a temporary expedient some restorers resort to modern products, which may make a piece of furniture look good now but will not last. Using products designed for the manufacture of new furniture to restore antique furniture should only be done if at all by a restorer with long experience.

The two materials with the biggest part to play are of course wood and glue.

WOOD

If the restorer needs to add material in order to repair a piece of furniture, he must select high-quality, dry, if possible old wood to ensure that his additions age in the same way as the wood of the original piece. Also old wood, having a patina already, will reduce to a minimum any colour matching that may be necessary.

Where material is needed to complete a piece of solid-wood furniture it is generally taken from somewhere else, i.e. from old beams or from other antique pieces of no interest (beech bed-frames for repairing chairs, which are often made of beech;

oak pieces, oak acquiring with age a colour that is difficult to imitate).

Veneer for repairs is sometimes also taken from old pieces, for example by sawing up the extension leaves of a nineteenth-century solid mahogany table. But plundering nineteenth-century furniture to repair the veneer on earlier pieces can be overdone, and the restorer should proceed with caution here; nineteenth-century furniture has had a very bad press and has been far too neglected.

The alternative is to use new veneer. The trade offers virtually no aged veneer any more – and nothing at all over thirty years old at most. Be that as it may, it is essential that restorers use only veneer that has been sawn by the traditional method. In the eighteenth century – as an engraving by the joiner Roubo tells us[2] – the log was placed upright and sawn with a rip-saw (ill. 11) used horizontally by two sawyers, which produced leaves of veneer of uneven thickness. This method was mechanized in the nineteenth century in the form of the rising wood saw with an alternating motion, powered originally by steam but nowadays by electricity. The upright log is fastened to a frame that stands in a pit 4 m deep. The motor drives the frame on the one hand, which rises to offer the log to the saw-blade, and on the other hand it moves the saw-blade backwards and forwards in the horizontal plane. This process gives leaves of veneer cut with the grain up to 4 m long and 0.70 m wide. It can also be used to saw at right angles to the grain, producing a cross-cut veneer (usually violet wood; ill. 8), or at a greater or lesser angle to the grain. The speed of the operation and the thickness of the leaf are both adjustable. Eighteenth-century saw-cut veneers were about 2 mm thick;[3] the usual thickness nowadays is 1.2 mm. Veneer is still sold by weight, and the restorer will usually buy at least two or four consecutive leaves in order of cutting so that he can complete symmetrical motifs.

Saw-cut veneer is now hard to come by; furniture manufacturers use very little of it, and restorers represent too small a market to justify producing it. In the Paris region, for example, there is only one firm left – with two saws, whereas before 1914 Paris boasted a hundred such machines – and in Paris itself there are very few shops selling saw-cut veneer, their field of activity extending abroad as well.

Some restorers, when they need only a small amount, saw their own veneer either by hand or with a band saw.

The veneer used by the trade nowadays is knife-cut either flat or on a rotary lathe. The log is first scalded or steamed to make it easier to cut. On the flat-slicing machine an alternating blade cuts leaves straight across the log; the rotary-cutting machine has a blade running parallel to the axis of the log, peeling the veneer off rather like a pencil-sharpener. The veneer obtained from both processes is subsequently dried artificially. For a variety of reasons it is unsuitable for use on antique furniture, although some self-styled restorers have been known to make use of it by gluing it to paper or cardboard in order to make up the required thickness. Modern veneer is in fact only $6/10$ or $7/10$ mm thick – a mere shaving. And the more beautiful the wood, the more thinly it is sliced. Used for restoration purposes, it will crack in a matter of months. Its colour deteriorates in consequence of the way the log has to be treated, and it cannot be stained satisfactorily to match an old colour. Saw-cut veneer, although more expensive than the knife-cut variety, does keep its colour because it has not been treated; and it can be worked without risk of perforating it, which means a saving of time.

Restocking, as I said, is very often a problem with veneer. Certain timbers used by inlayers in centuries gone by are no longer obtainable. Is this going to stop one restoring a particular piece of furniture? As far as indigenous varieties are concerned, certain fruit-tree timbers are becoming hard to find and dyed timbers are problematical. Grey-dyed maple is impossible to get hold of. Timbers dyed green and black are still available on the Italian market but only in knife-cut veneers. Consequently restorers have to do their own green dying, using for example pear wood, hornbeam, plane or sycamore. Some dyes, however, we can no longer produce because the methods have been lost.[4]

Most exotic timbers come from South America – Brazil in particular – or Africa. Some of them, e.g. violet wood or king-wood, are still available but in nothing like the splendid quality they used to come in, especially from Guiana. Others have become very rare, e.g. Brazilian rosewood and snake-wood, or have disappeared from the market altogether; they still exist, but there is not the demand to make it worth while exploiting them. Amboyna and thuya burr are unobtainable. Cuban mahogany – the best there is – has not been exported for a long time; all the mahogany nowadays comes from Mexico, Honduras and Africa. Ebony comes from India – this is the best – or Gabon.

Once they have been cut, the leaves of veneer are stored flat in a slightly humid atmosphere, the position to prevent buckling and the humidity to prevent splitting.

GLUE

Two types of glue are available to the restorer: natural, animal glue, as used traditionally in cabinet-making, and synthetic adhesives (ills. 9–10). It might almost be said to be a principle of restoring that one only uses the former.

Animal glue or Scotch glue, as it is sometimes called, is made by boiling abattoir and tannery waste. The bouillon, homogenized by filtration, solidifies in the form of gelatine, which is then cut into slabs and dried on grilles; it can also be solidified in pearl or granular form. A good-quality glue will be transparent and uniform in colour, will swell up in water, and will thicken when heated. There are two types: that made from bones and that made from skin and sinews. Their properties are complementary, and they are usually mixed before use in the proportion of two slabs of bone glue to one of sinew. Animal glue is also available ready-mixed.

Animal glue should never be used fresh, when its power of adhesion is unsatisfactory, but only several months after being prepared in the following fashion. The slabs are broken up and left to soak in cold water in a copper vessel overnight (pearl glue need only be soaked for twenty to thirty minutes). The glue absorbs a certain percentage of water and swells up. The surplus water is poured off and the glue heated in a double boiler till it melts. It will need to be skimmed from time to time, but the most important thing is that it should not be allowed to boil. When it reaches the consistency of gelatine it is moulded, dried and cut up into cakes. Animal glue is used warm. When he needs some the restorer places enough for about a week in a glue pot (ill. 10) and melts it down in a double boiler. It quickly deteriorates and loses its properties when heated

too violently or too often, and it must be thrown away as soon as it begins to blacken.

Whenever possible, glue should be spread on both the surfaces to be joined. At the time pressure is applied the glue should be still warm or, if not, reheated; otherwise it will not adhere properly. A joint that is being glued can be kept warm with a blowlamp, whereas in veneering the glue is reheated with a veneering iron or hot caul (see pp. 61–2). Heat has the effect of softening glue that was beginning to congeal. Hardening of the glue, which is what produces adhesion between the two surfaces, takes place as it gradually cools. Animal glue sets quickly, but pressure must be maintained for a minimum of twelve hours.

Animal glue has the inestimable advantage of allowing corrections to be made. If in the course of restoring a piece the restorer notices that an element has been badly glued, he can always reheat the glue and do the job again. When regluing veneer one can sometimes even re-use the original glue by warming it with a hot iron applied on top of a damping cloth (see p. 62). Furthermore it is reversible; two elements held together by this means can always be separated again if necessary by future restorers, using either alcohol or the damping cloth and hot iron method, which can be done so quickly as to avoid any damage to the wood.

9
Animal glue.
Top: slabs of clear, transparent bone glue.
Centre: slabs of sinew glue, smaller and dried on closer grilles; the glue is more brown and opaque.
Bottom left: slab of mixed glue.
Bottom right: animal glue in pearl form.

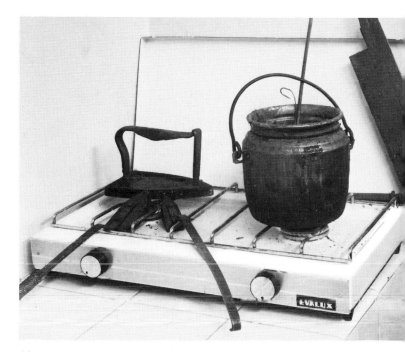

10
Copper glue pot. This consists of two vessels, the one that contains the glue resting in another one. Glue keeps better when heated by gas than when heated electrically.

Regrettably some restorers have given up using animal glue because of the preparation involved and because it means they have to work fast and use heat sources. Another thing against it is the difficulty of obtaining good glue in the first place. Nowadays gelatine is primarily reserved for foodstuffs and the photographic industry. Animal glue is virtually unobtainable except in pearl or granular form, and it no longer has the power of adhesion that it used to have. As in the case of saw-cut veneer, many restorers are living on their stocks of old glue.

Fish glue, which is made from the skin, bones and swimming-bladders of certain fish, is still used

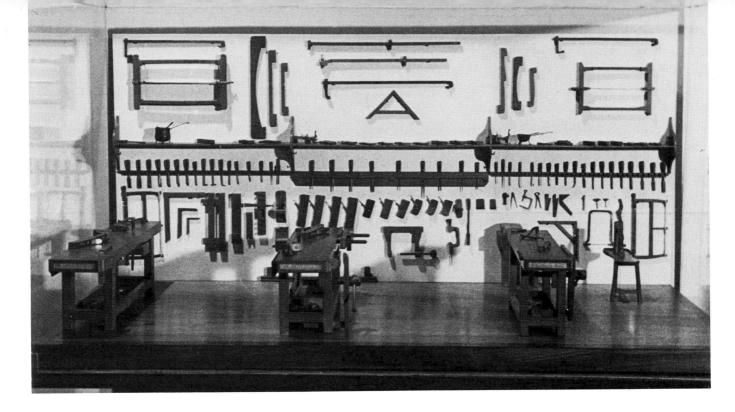

11
Model of a joinery shop. Commissioned by Mme de Genlis for the education of the children of the Duke of Orléans and made by the Périer brothers in Paris *c.* 1783. Top left and right: rip-saw. Bottom right: marquetry cramp (Paris, Musée du Conservatoire national des Arts et Métiers).

occasionally, particularly for gluing joints. Applied cold or warm, it has a very long setting time (a day, even several days) and is also subject to diminishing quality and inadequate supply.

MODERN ADHESIVES
Because of these difficulties some restorers have decided to go over to synthetic-resin adhesives, whose power of adhesion is extremely high.

Vinyl adhesives such as Alcamer, with a polyvinyl-acetate base, are sold ready for use in the form of a white liquid. They can be used cold, and they leave more time for adjustments. They set by elimination of the solvents contained in them, and pressure need be applied only for a few hours (not less than two).

Partisans of vinyl adhesives regard them as better adapted to the conditions of modern life than animal glue. But if they can be used quite conveniently to glue porous timbers such as mahogany or snake-wood, they are less effective on the greasy timbers often found in antique furniture – rosewood, violet wood, Brazilian rosewood, etc. They are also acid, which can have disastrous consequences, and they are highly sensitive to damp. The acids used for dyeing pieces of new veneer have more effect on vinyl adhesives than on animal glue

24

12
Model of a joinery shop. Louis-Edme Fernon, joiner at Tonnerre, 1821 (38 by 43 by 20 cm). Top: wooden hand cramps. On the bench: trying plane, smoothing plane, glue pot and water level (Tonnerre, Musée municipal).

the piece of furniture concerned; the process involves moistening the wood and damaging the veneer or the joints, which means that the restorer has to renew elements that were sound before his intervention.

One does not want to reject synthetic adhesives out of hand, however, when they can make the job easier without risk. Indeed restorers say they are quite happy with some of them, having managed to adapt their use to the needs of restoration. But this involves making tests and being very careful about innovating. Vinyl adhesives can for example be used to glue non-ferrous metals (see p. 90) and also to fix a piece that does not form part of a joint and will consequently never need to be unglued. Plastic wood products can likewise be a boon to the restorer.

in terms of reducing their power of adhesion. Finally, vinyl adhesives are completely unsuitable for regluing veneer piece by piece by the hammer method (see p. 60).

Some restorers have also been tempted to use epoxy adhesives of the Araldite type, which consist of a resin and a hardening agent. Welding rather than gluing, they can be used to join a wide range of materials.

Synthetic adhesives are generally harmful in restoration because of their finality. They can only be unglued with great difficulty and to the detriment of

Tools

Restoration is essentially manual work, and even where a particular job could be done on a machine it is often quicker to do it by hand. But the necessary tools (ills. 11–13) do pose problems in that they are either no longer manufactured, in which case the restorer must try to get hold of them second-hand, or will need to be imported from abroad. For example the French restorer needing certain tools used for sculpture will have to buy them in England, because they are no longer manufactured in France, while he will have to make a trip to Switzerland in order to equip himself with the three-cornered files needed for cutting the teeth of marquetry-saw blades.

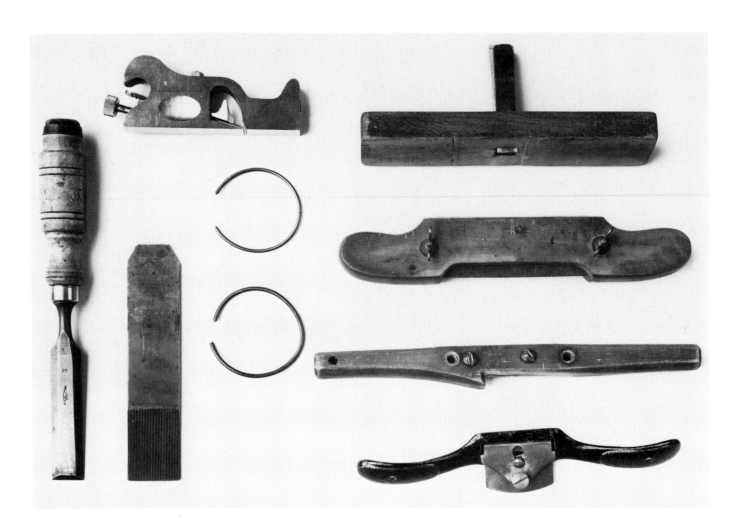

13
Joinery tools. Left to right and top to bottom: chisel, 'rebate' plane (with an iron as wide as the stock), toothing-plane iron, springs used for pressing small glue jobs, router plane (for making the bottoms of slots uniform), scraper, moulding plane (for mouldings and strings, the appropriate blade being inserted in the stock as required), spokeshave (a two-handled plane).

Causes

Damage to antique furniture comes essentially from the wood itself, though it may also be due to faulty manufacture, careless maintenance or bad restoration.

Wood, like paper, cotton and tobacco, is a hygroscopic material, that is to say that variations in the water content of the surrounding air cause it to lose or absorb moisture. Wood is made up of cells. In the case of conifers, where the cells are known as tracheids, they serve both to give wood its consistency and to conduct water. The more complex cells of deciduous woods include fibres that provide rigidity and water-carrying vessels that in certain types are visible with the naked eye (as pores).[1] Wood always contains a certain quantity of water, both inside the cells (free water) and in the cell walls (impregnation water). This water content is expressed as a percentage of the dry weight of the wood. Once timber has been felled and converted, its free water evaporates in the natural process of drying. With the free water gone, the wood is said to be at 'fibre saturation point', which corresponds to a moisture content of about 30%. No play has occurred as yet. Below this point it is the turn of the impregnation water to evaporate, and the wood continues to dry out until it is what is known as 'air dry', at which point the moisture levels of the wood and the surrounding atmosphere are in equilibrium. The average level of this moisture balance or hygroscopic balance in Europe is 15%. Each type of atmosphere, however, as determined by a particular temperature and degree of relative humidity, calls for a different moisture balance level in wood: as the atmosphere changes, the wood adapts itself to the requisite level.

When the air is so dry as to cause the water in the cell walls to evaporate, those membranes shrink. The sum of their shrinkages represents the total shrinkage of the piece of wood, which will now have altered in size. Shrinkage occurs at right angles to the grain, not along the grain, and is approximately twice as great tangentially as radially (fig. 13). This unequal distribution of shrinkage accounts for the distortions to which wood is subject. A board cut towards the heart of the trunk ('on the quarter', as it is called) will shrink without distor-

27

tion; a board cut tangentially ('slab-cut') will camber because the edges will dry out more than the centre (fig. 14). On the other hand, if wood absorbs moisture it swells. Swelling and shrinkage account for the phenomenon known as 'play'. Wood is never stable but continues to exhibit play as the atmosphere changes. Shrinkage potential, which varies according to the type of wood, is high in such deciduous hardwoods as oak – and higher still in beech – middling in conifers, and low in walnut and mahogany. Shrinkage can give rise to splits or fissures.

As far as furniture is concerned, the protection afforded by paint or varnish puts a brake on moisture exchanges but does not block them entirely. In the old days, during the winter, wood used to 'breathe' by swelling at night and shrinking during the day, when the temperature went up; wood fires, even when the fuel is dry, give off humidity as a result of the sap. Nowadays, in the constant temperature provided by central heating, wood shrinks all the time. Underfloor heating is particularly detrimental in this respect. In this kind of very dry atmosphere, where temperatures average 22°C and relative humidity 30 to 40%, the moisture level in the furniture may drop as low as 6 or 7%. In summer, with the windows open, more humid air comes in from outside and pushes the moisture level of the wood up to 12 or 13%. In the modern apartment, then, wood is subject to continuous play. Whereas the wood used in the manufacture of modern furniture is artificially dried to a very low moisture level (8–10%) unobtainable by the traditional method of air-drying, antique furniture is clearly not suited to withstand such fluctuations. Consequently it sustains a certain amount of

damage – worse in our century than ever before. Where it is not glued, i.e. in a tongue and groove joint, the wood of a piece of furniture has free play, but where such play is blocked it may in certain types of wood build up enough pressure to burst glued joints. In pinned joints, the pins may shrink and slip out. A piece of furniture may be found to have suffered worst on the side that was nearest a window or radiator.

Other types of damage may threaten the cohesion of a piece of furniture, e.g. internal splits due to poor felling, or knots (showing where branches emerged) that, since they do not shrink like the wood around them, may come to stick out on the carcases of veneered furniture. Moreover, wood is susceptible to attack by a variety of parasites (see p. 30).

And of course poor-quality manufacture may also have serious consequences as regards the life of a piece of furniture. Antique furniture, even the more pretentious kinds, is sometimes not very stoutly made, which has always been a cause of occasionally exaggerated complaint. Roubo castigated the furniture manufacturers of his day for doing their job 'with as little of fashioning or material as anyhow possible',[2] and not long afterwards Mercier made this virulent attack on Parisian upholsterers and furniture dealers: 'A fellow will sell you a secretaire that falls apart after three weeks. You have bought a wardrobe, you say? Wait the month out and it will shed its panels. There are pieces coming from their shops that are but phantoms: give them twenty days and they are rickety, crumbling, worm-eaten wrecks.'[3] Burty, writing at the time of the Second Empire, echoed these gloomy sentiments in relation to the output of his own day: 'Moreover everything conspires to bring about a

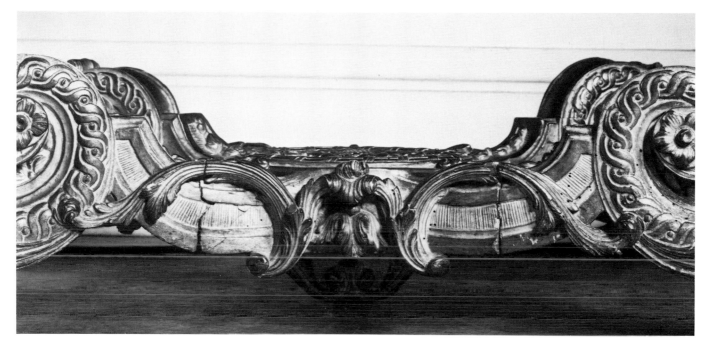

constant lowering of manufacturing standards: the new price laws that tyrannically apply even to essentials, the speed of manufacture dictated by the feverish pace of modern life, and the poor quality of modern timbers, which are cut from younger trees and allowed less time to lie in store and draw the benefit of gradual drying.'[4]

Subsequent neglect aggravates these defects, whether arising out of everyday use, transportation, disastrous maintenance, changes of fashion that condemn certain pieces to exile in store-rooms, or simply poor positioning, e.g. prolonged exposure to the bleaching action of the sun and – even more dangerous – of the moon.[5]

Without wishing to labour the point that much of antique furniture has been deliberately mutilated in order to make it more useful or more fashionable, or because no one knew how to restore it, I must

14
A common accident. The stretcher of a console table has split under the weight of the middle portion.

stress once more that the damage most difficult to put right is that resulting from previous interventions. These range from the unwelcome attentions of the servant who has dropped a clock – 'It is only a little cupid whose legs have got bent, but a wallop with the hammer will soon fix that'[6] – to restoration work carried out by poor craftsmen who proceeded either dangerously, by using too much potassium stripper or rubbing down veneer too fiercely (see pp. 35, 67), or clumsily, for example by renewing portions in the wrong kind of wood (ill. 34) or planing off the top of the leg of a commode that had not shrunk like the rest and perhaps removing the manufacturer's mark in the process.

These are the sorts of reason why a piece of furniture may fetch up in the restorer's workshop. Different types of damage occur in solid-wood and veneered furniture. The former is more susceptible to worm, for example. Chairs suffer particularly because they are used a great deal and because they are often re-upholstered many times. Before working on them the restorer has them de-upholstered by a professional upholsterer, who must be careful not to leave any tacks in because if these were hit at the re-upholstery stage they would split the wood.

The carcases of veneered furniture call for the same sorts of cabinet-making repair as solid-wood furniture, the difference being that a solid-wood piece with a natural finish is more difficult to repair inconspicuously than a veneered piece.

The furniture restorer heats his workshop to between 18 and 20 °C, and he works by daylight, in which he can best distinguish the colour of the wood he is treating. It goes without saying that, if he has to lay a piece of veneered furniture on its side, he will keep it off the floor with a carpet, a piece of clean canvas, or suitable chocks. A piece that has been varnished will need to be protected from knocks, for example by covering it with a woollen blanket. Another point to bear in mind is that, whether one is stripping, staining, or whatever it is, as soon as one comes across a case that is at all tricky it is essential to make tests first.

Rot and worm damage

There are various destructive agents that threaten wood with rot or worm damage, the sap-wood or soft outer part of the trunk being particularly susceptible.

Rot is caused by fungi, the most common and dangerous of which is the merulius or house fungus. This feeds on the cellular membranes of wood, causing it gradually to disintegrate. Merulius needs a certain level of humidity in order to flourish, so that rot occurs particularly in a damp environment. Worm damage is caused by certain insects – various small *coleoptera*, termites – that appear to be more widespread nowadays than they were. Of the former, the most common enemies of furniture are the beetles of the *anobiidae* family. Some species of this insect will only attack wood that a fungus has already started on. Others go for sound wood of almost any kind but particularly fruit-tree woods, walnut and beech; they steer clear of Cuban mahogany but will attack other types of mahogany. The beetles may be anything from 2 to 7 mm long, depending on the species, and live for three or four years. They lay their eggs on the surface of wood, in joints or fissures, between May and September. The eggs hatch quickly, and the larvae, which actually feed on wood, bore galleries in it that are afterwards full of wood dust. There may be no indication on the surface of the wood that anything is wrong. Pupation occurs just below the surface, and the adult insect emerges in spring by boring a round hole between 1 and 4 mm in diameter (mistakenly known as a 'worm hole'), the dust from which is one's first sign that the piece is infected. In other words, whereas a piece of furniture with 'worm holes' may no longer contain any insects, one with no visible holes may already be under attack. The adult insects often lay on the same piece of furniture as they have escaped from, possibly even in or near their own exit holes. In fact they are fairly static creatures altogether, hence the steadily worsening state of the infected piece and the contamination of neighbouring pieces.

Other *coleoptera* of similar habits produce equally disastrous results. The lyctid or powder-post beetle is tempted only by large-vesseled woods such as oak, since it lays its eggs inside the vessels. The capricorn beetle, which flourishes in hot, dry conditions, prefers conifers. Its larvae make an audible sound as they bore. The insect continues to live in wood in the adult stage, usually without producing any external evidence of its ravages.

It is the same with wood infested by termites. Termites are not strictly speaking wood insects; it is just that they feed mainly on cellulose material and find this particularly in wood, in which they bore galleries containing no wood dust. They are native to hot countries, but no doubt as a result of the general increase of domestic heating over the last fifty years or more, they have become established at various points in Europe, namely in parts of Hamburg and Paris and in the south and south-west of France.

There are three aspects to the treatment of rot and worm damage: disinfection, consolidation and prevention.

DISINFECTION

Clearly any infected piece of furniture must be treated immediately because of the risk of contamination. There is no ideal, once-and-for-all remedy. A variety of methods is currently available: treatment with commercial insecticides, formolizing, gas impregnation, irradiation, or, if the wood also needs consolidating, infiltration with a synthetic resin.

Treatment with insecticide

Various chlorine-based liquid insecticides are available commercially.[7] They are either brushed on or injected into the holes with a syringe.[8] This is best done between October and April, when the insects are in the larval or pupal stages. The treatment has some disadvantages. For example, insecticide must not be applied to a surface that is to be glued, because the glue will no longer grip. Commercial insecticides are sticky and darken wood. When injected with a syringe, they leave a 'halo' around the holes unless great care is taken (ill. 15); overflows must be avoided or mopped up quickly. Insecticide

15
Chair arm attacked by woodworm. Insecticide injected into the holes has left stains around the openings.

stains may last for several years but do eventually evaporate.

Consequently it is best to use these products only on the non-visible parts of a piece, i.e. on the back, the bottom, the inside, or, if the piece has been dismantled, on places that will be hidden when it is reassembled. The rest of the piece will be impregnated by the fumes given off. The best way of going about it is to inject insecticide into the holes and 'back up' by brushing it all over the non-visible surfaces. But the restorer who is pressed for time may confine himself to brushing. A longer-lasting result will be obtained if the treatment is repeated two or three years in succession.

Formolizing

Some restorers prefer to use Formol, a liquid that smells very strong but does not stain. It too is applied with brush or syringe, and it can be used on veneer. The smell disappears very quickly.

The remaining solutions are relatively modern and represent adaptations of industrial processes to the treatment of works of art.

Gas impregnation

Certain highly toxic gases, which need to be used with extreme care, are used for disinfection on a large scale. The process can be applied to furniture. It is done in a gas chamber, which is filled with methyl bromide (particularly dangerous to humans) or ethylene oxide. Gas impregnation provides a quick cure but affords no protection against subsequent attack.

Radio sterilization

Gamma radiation has excellent penetration and is fatal to living organisms; it is used, for example, to sterilize medical equipment. The infected piece of furniture is exposed to a radiation source for about an hour, which has the effect of killing fungi, eggs, larvae and adult insects. The process offers the advantage of disinfecting the wood without impregnating it with chemicals. It does, however, involve some risk to the structure of the material itself.

CONSOLIDATION

The disinfected wood may, if it is very badly damaged, need consolidating. This is where it becomes difficult for the restorer to abide by the golden rule of reversibility.

Up to now cavities were always filled with natural consolidating agents – either wax or a mixture of glue and whiting. Arising out of research conducted over the last few years, there are now synthetic resins that both kill parasites and consolidate wood. They are used on archaeological finds, saturated wood, wood carvings and, if necessary, on furniture. Following such treatment, the piece is heavier than before but also very much more solid and possibly in less danger of being attacked again because of the way the plastic hardens it.

There are two ways of going about this:

In the first, the resin[9] in its solvent is introduced into the holes in the surface of the wood either with a syringe or by the drip method. The drip method allows more control, and it is in fact important to keep impregnation to a minimum if the wood is to retain its structure and flexibility and not actually 'become' plastic. Any resin that overflows on to the surface of the piece is removed immediately with solvent. When treatment is completed – and it takes a very long time – the piece is left for several weeks for the solvent to evaporate. As it does so, the resin hardens and stiffens the wood. If impregnation has been kept within reasonable limits the wood can still be worked and restored normally afterwards. On gilded and painted furniture the resin acts as an adhesive to refix the ground and any flaking portions, and it appears to have no effect on the colours of painted wood.

The second process, developed at the Nuclear Research Centre, Grenoble, is much quicker. It is also used for stone, and it comprises two phases. After cleaning (and de-upholstering, in the case of a chair or settee) and a check that the piece of furniture does not use any vinyl adhesive (which would be dissolved), it is placed in an air-tight cylindrical tank 3.20 m long and 0.80 m in diameter and subjected to a vacuum. Liquid resin is then introduced to cover the piece, which it penetrates in depth by way of the pores and galleries. After a few hours the cylinder is emptied. The piece is then placed in an irradiation chamber and the resin hardened by means of gamma radiation, this second phase of the operation also lasting for a matter of hours. The weight of the piece may then be twice what it was at the beginning of the operation. It will no longer feel like wood, and it will be impossible to work with ordinary tools. A chair, for example, will be very difficult to re-upholster because the tacks will hardly go in. Owing to the fact that the surface of the wood, whether natural or painted, will darken in colour and the wood itself shrink, cracking any gilding or paintwork, this second process is unsuitable for painted or gilded furniture, especially since it fails to refix any flaking portions. In fact its disadvantages as regards treating furniture inevitably limit its use to natural wood furniture that is in a truly parlous state.

Furthermore, furniture treated by modern scientific methods needs very watchful after-care. Wood impregnated in this way is not stabilized for good but remains sensitive to climatic variation; any play, however, is blocked by the plastic. One is dealing with a heterogeneous material, and there is no way of telling how it will behave. So the piece will need to be kept in an even more carefully controlled environment than an untreated piece.

Synthetic resin consolidation does indeed offer a spectacular short-term remedy for works that are apparently beyond saving. We must keep a sense of proportion, however, and for the time being its use must remain exceptional. Years of experimentation are necessary to establish what consequences resins have before they can come into more systematic use.

PREVENTION

The wax or varnish with which most furniture is covered already affords some protection. The powder-post beetle, for example, cannot attack waxed or varnished wood because the pores are plugged (see p. 31). Another solution is to use commercial insecticides, which though they may be inadequate for the purposes of cure offer an excellent mode of protection. If a piece is treated in February or March, i.e. before swarming time, the insects born in the wood will, in boring their exit holes, come up against an insecticide barrier and die within a few hours. This treatment can be repeated every two or three years. In some places (museum store-rooms, for example) a useful precaution is to spread some paradichlorobenzene.

WOODWORK

Stripping gilding and paintwork

Restoring a piece of furniture often involves stripping off a surface coating that has been applied to decorate or protect the piece. The purpose of stripping (ill. 67) is not always the same, nor is it always done at the same stage of the restoration process; different types of furniture call for a different order of events. Veneers are usually stripped after consolidation (see p. 52). On gilded or painted solid wood, however, if what is needed is a liquid stripper that may make the wood swell up and any glued joints come apart, stripping is done before regluing or reassembly. It is only done at all in very specific cases (see p. 96): either to get back to the bare wood when this has been covered with modern paintwork or gilding of no interest, or to get back to the original gilding or paintwork where this has been covered up with subsequent coats – and here the job calls for particular care. Only the professional restorer can judge which solution to adopt.

DRY STRIPPING
This process, involving long and meticulous work with carving tools (ill. 71), makes it possible to uncover old paintwork or gilding that has been covered up and also to remove water gilding and glue-based paintwork.[1] The ground used in the two latter cases is also removed, and since this contains glue it will be difficult to get off; the restorer may have to wet it with hot water and take a brush to it.

CHEMICAL STRIPPING
One can buy ready-mixed liquid chemical strippers in the shops. They contain acetone, which does the actual stripping, and glycerine, which stops them evaporating too fast. They rid wood of oil-paint, mordant gilding, and bronze gilding with a turpentine or varnish base,[2] but they do not attack water gilding or glue-based paint. If the material to be removed is obstinate, the stripper can be hardened by adding a small quantity of potassium to it.

HOT-WATER STRIPPING
This is used on water gilding and glue-based paint. The restorer soaks some sawdust in hot water and, wearing gloves, applies it to the wood and winds on flannel bandages to hold it there. The sawdust is to conduct the moisture, to maintain which it is best to place the piece in a damp atmosphere. The restorer

34

remoistens the sawdust a number of times, keeping an eye on the results. Eventually the glue will break up, and the restorer finishes the job with carving tools.

POTASSIUM STRIPPING

When the object is to expose the wood, the quickest method is to use a potassium stripper. This can, however, seriously jeopardize the piece of furniture being treated. Potassium burns and blackens the surface of wood, attacks it in depth, cracks it, and tends to linger on in the latent state. Moreover it has to be rinsed off, and this will make the wood swell.[3] So it is only to be used with the greatest caution, and the piece must be dried very thoroughly. The best procedure is to leave a protective coat on the wood and scrape this off afterwards.

A potassium stripper can be made up with potassium extract, which comes in liquid form, and an admixture of whiting, flour, or sawdust to form a paste. Again wearing gloves, the restorer dabs this on with a nylon brush. The paste softens the coats of paint; it is left to work for two hours, then the piece is rinsed under running water and the paint removed with a scrubbing-brush – not, repeat not, with a wire brush. The occasional bits that stick, particularly in the hollows, can be removed with carving tools afterwards – very carefully if the piece of furniture is to be waxed, less so if it is to be primed for repainting or regilding. Immediately after rinsing, the wood is treated with oxalic, hydrochloric or acetic acid (see p. 72) to lighten it and at the same time remove the grease. Then it must be rinsed again with a hog-bristle brush (the acid would decompose a nylon brush). If necessary the treatment is repeated, either immediately if the

16
Repairs to the inside of a Louis XIV commode that could not be dismantled. A split between the two boards making up the right-hand side has been plugged with in-fills and a large block has been glued with its grain lying at right angles to the joint in order to prevent the split from reappearing. A series of smaller blocks lying along the grain of the panel strengthens the structure lower down.

35

17
Straightening a cambered panel by means of in-fills inserted parallel to the grain. The handwritten label glued to the back of this late fifteenth-century *tarsia certosina* panel proves that the restoration was carried out in Italy during the nineteenth century. Note the double dovetail key at bottom left.

wood is very sound, or after a two-day drying period to let it recover its consistency.

Once stripping is completed, the restorer leaves the piece to dry for about a fortnight – longer if the wood is worm-eaten and has consequently absorbed more water – before going on to restore or re-prime it.

Dismantling

A piece of furniture, as I have said, should only be dismantled if it has to be; in particular dismantling should be kept to a minimum in the case of veneered, painted or gilt pieces in order not to damage their appearance. Solid-wood furniture can always be dismantled, whether its joints are glued or, as with certain chairs, for example, merely pinned with dowels. Veneered furniture, which is always glued, is often difficult to take apart, and in some cases the restorer will be wise to resign himself to carrying out repairs inside the piece as it stands (ill. 16). Certain works reproduce structural systems borrowed from antique furniture, which may make them easier to dismantle,[4] but every master craftsman used to have his own methods of manufacture.

Mortise and tenon joints glued with animal glue can be undone by injecting 95° surgical spirit with a syringe (methylated spirit will not do). Alcohol does not make wood warp. It works not by dissolving the glue but by crystallizing it. After a moment the restorer starts gently working the joint to and fro; it must be eased rather than jerked open, and more spirit must be added if it resists. Eventually a tap with a mallet will separate the two pieces. Marking the pieces carefully, the restorer then scrapes the old glue out of the mortises and cleans them with chisel, rasp and toothing plane, helping out if need be with a brush dipped in hot water. The tenons must not be rubbed down as this would reduce their thickness.

Dowels are not glued – unless mistakenly by a previous restorer – and they are removed with a dowel punch. If they resist they are drilled through the middle and removed piece by piece with a narrow-gauge chisel.

Distortion

The wood may have cambered or assumed a spiral warp. Although straightening distorted wood is difficult if not impossible, the following methods are sometimes used.

If the camber is not too pronounced, parallel saw-cuts are made in the concave side and long thin wedge-shaped in-fills inserted with the grain,[5] which help to straighten the panel (ill. 17). A spiral warp can be corrected by using the same method on part of the piece only.

Sometimes the restorer will prefer to moisten a piece of distorted wood and heat it with smoothing irons or in a fume chamber[6] before putting it in a press. The distortion may reappear afterwards, however, and to avoid this the wood, once dry, can be held with a veneer panel of the appropriate thickness glued to one or both sides (e.g. in the case of shelves) or with blocks (see p. 43) fixed with their grain at right angles to that of the distorted piece.

Filling

It is often necessary to fill small holes, including worm holes, on solid parts of pieces of furniture or to level off an area of groundwork before regluing the veneer. This is usually done with putty of some sort, although putty repairs can be overdone and it is better to use wood wherever possible.

Small holes used to be filled with wax, which is often found to have darkened on solid-wood furniture, or with a mixture of whiting and glue, which has the disadvantage of shrinking as it dries, leaving a further gap that needs to be filled in a second stage. Nowadays one can buy plastic wood, which comes either ready-mixed or as two separate ingredients, namely powdered wood and a liquid synthetic resin. Every restorer has his favourite brand; what one wants is a high-quality product that is not going to shrink. The two ingredients are mixed to the appropriate consistency as and when required, and on solid-wood furniture the mixture may be tinted with powder colour to match the original wood. Mixing triggers off the hardening process. The product is applied with a spatula, and since it is very fast-setting, particularly when applied thickly, it needs to be levelled off before it dries out completely (which it does about a quarter of an hour after application). Left any later, this operation becomes very difficult and involves a risk of damaging the surrounding surface. Liquid wood does in fact become extremely hard and adheres very powerfully – two advantages that may equally well be disadvantages. Ordinary animal glue can be used to stick veneer on top of it.

This extreme rigidity of plastic wood makes it unsuitable for use in certain cases. Wax is less hard and is sometimes better for carved furniture. Used on the rebates of chair seats or for filling any holes left by upholstery nails (see p. 45), plastic wood would make it impossible for the upholsterer to drive in any new nails. In such cases the restorer uses a more flexible fill made of vinyl adhesive and sawdust, which he applies in two stages. The mixture is first introduced in a fairly liquid form to allow it to penetrate well. It is then left to dry for 48 hours. It will shrink a bit, so the operation is then repeated with a rather thicker mixture, which is also left to dry for 48 hours before being rubbed down. Strips of canvas may be glued over the filled surfaces for extra solidity.

Filling dents

A piece of furniture may have received a blow or scratch that has compressed the wood fibres, which must then be made to swell back up to their previous state. This is done by covering the affected area with a thick damp cloth and standing a hot iron on it. The steam makes the wood underneath swell up, and the operation is continued for as long as necessary. Alternatively the dent can be subjected for a time to a daily dose of hot water. Special care must be taken with veneered furniture not to unglue the veneer by these methods. In the case of scratches on varnished finishes, these must be rubbed down and revarnished, although a scratch that seems to disappear when rubbed down may reappear at the varnishing stage.

Repairing tenons

A defective tenon may still be usable, or it may not. Sometimes a tenon will sit too loosely in its mortise, either because it has shrunk and is now too thin, or because the glue has been removed from the joint. Loose tenons need to be reinforced by gluing an extra thickness on to them. Where the dowels fixing the joint together have split the tenon or the cheeks of the mortise, the damaged places are reinforced with dovetails; once the joint has been reassembled, these are drilled to admit the dowels (fig. 1).

When a tenon is beyond repair it is replaced with a false tenon (see p. 40) or – an even more solid solution – with a comb tenon. In the latter case the restorer begins by flushing off the place where the old tenon was attached. Taking a piece of wood of the thickness of the old tenon, he cuts two or three teeth in it and shapes them into pins (see p. 42); he then drills two or three holes in the flushed-off surface to take the pins. The comb tenon is now ready to take the place of the old tenon (fig. 2). On a piece of mahogany furniture, since mahogany has a tendency to split, the restorer will make the new tenon of beech.

Splits

Splits may be of two kinds. Either they occur in the body of a piece of wood, in which case they are irregular in shape; or they appear between two boards that were originally joined but have shrunk apart, as happens on desk lids, for example, or on the sides of a carcase when this is made up of several boards, or between a cross-piece and an upright. Furthermore the split may affect only the surface or it may go right through.

If the element in which the split has occurred can be dismantled, the restorer does so. He then prolongs the line of the split with a saw in order to separate the two parts completely, where this has not already occurred. Using a toothing plane, he cleans up the two sides of the split and levels them off where necessary. He then glues them together and holds them in a clamp, possibly reinforcing the mend by one of the methods described in the next section (false tongue, one or more pins, one or more keys) or by using blocks. With the split closed up, the piece of wood will probably no longer be big enough for the space it is meant to fill; there will be a gap of the length and breadth of the split as it was, which the restorer will fill by gluing on a flush making-out piece of the required size (fig. 3). On a tongue-and-groove panel the making-out piece can be concealed in one of the grooves. On solid-wood furniture, if the making-out piece is going to be visible the restorer will use the same wood as the piece of furniture is made of; on veneered furniture he will use a wood similar to that of the carcase.

If this method is impracticable, i.e. particularly if the piece cannot be dismantled, the restorer inserts an in-fill to plug the split. In-fills are used above all to repair the carcases of veneered furniture, where the repair will be covered up by the facing. The wood of the in-fill must lie along the grain, and preferably it will be of the same kind as the piece of furniture. Inserting it is a delicate operation. The first step is to even up the place where it is to go. If it is to fill a joint that has opened, the sides of the gap will already be straight and flat and will only need cleaning. In other cases the restorer widens the split slightly with a hand saw in order to straighten the sides. If the split is only a shallow one it need not be opened up right through the wood; the restorer simply cuts a groove by hand (chisel) or with a machine to make the sides and bottom of the split even, the cross-section of the groove being determined by that of the in-fill to be inserted. This may be rectangular, slightly scarfed to give it better adhesion (fig. 4 B²). If there is a danger of this type of in-fill giving rise to fresh splits at its two bottom corners, the restorer will choose instead one with a wide-angle section like those used by restorers of wooden panel paintings (fig. 4 B³). In certain cases the restorer will insert in-fills from both sides (fig. 4 B⁴). If the wood is split right through, a more solid repair can be obtained with two in-fills scarfed in opposite directions and inserted simultaneously

18
Plugging splits that have appeared in the bottom of a drawer by gluing strips of canvas on the outside.

under a certain amount of pressure (fig. 4 B⁵). Where the line of the split is not straight, several in-fills are inserted end to end. Thin glue is applied to the split and to the sides of the in-fill, and the latter is inserted by hand and pressed between two blocks. Many restorers regard the in-fill as an ineffective and temporary measure; it will not last, they feel, and before long the split will reappear. If this does occur, however, it is often due to the in-fill not fitting properly. At any rate, avoiding as it does the need for dismantling, it is the right remedy in certain cases.

Sometimes a split can be plugged quite conveniently with plastic wood – when it has only just begun, for example, or when it is so crooked that in-fills would be difficult to fit properly. This is very quickly done; if the split goes right through, one side is stopped up with adhesive tape and the resin is simply poured or squeezed in.

Any pieces added to veneered furniture are going to increase the surface area of the carcase, and when the restorer comes to glue the facing back on he will have to cheat slightly by adding a strip of veneer of the same size as the in-fill or making-out piece, or two narrower strips, one on each side. This is a particularly tricky operation when one is dealing with shaped panels. In the case of mahogany-veneered furniture, the restorer uses solid mahogany for anything added to the carcase; it will then match the veneer when this is replaced.

A split on a non-visible part of a piece of furniture (the back, the bottom, etc.) need not be closed up or plugged; one will simply seal it by gluing a piece of canvas over the outside in order to keep out the dust (ill. 18).

Consolidating joints and gluings

When it comes to consolidating the joint between two elements that have come apart, preventing a split from recurring, or adding a fresh element, the restorer uses a variety of methods, sometimes in combination. Some of them, being invisible, are mostly used on solid-wood furniture; others are better for veneered furniture, where they can be covered up. A few of these methods are controversial, some restorers claiming that they mutilate the piece of furniture being treated. But their use will depend on the problem to be solved; each one of them, depending on the circumstances, may be either inevitable or impracticable. The various strengthening pieces used are glued and then pressed; they must be selected from sound wood to avoid contaminating the rest of the piece.

JOINTS IN THE THICKNESS OF THE WOOD

These very solid types of joint are used for fixing two elements together by means of a third, added element.

A *false tongue* (fig. 5) is used for a straight joint. The restorer makes a groove in the thickness of the wood running the whole length of the two faces to be joined. He then beds into these grooves and glues there a piece of cross-grain wood or plywood (5 mm gauge, if there is enough thickness to take it). Other strengthening pieces used do not occupy the whole length of the joint.

The *false tenon* (fig. 6) works on the same principle as the false tongue except that it joins two mortises. *Pins* or dowels (fig. 7; ill. 20), circular in section, are much used for joining broken pieces or refixing the bottom of a leg, for example. They need not be of the same wood as the piece of furniture; what matters is that they should lie with the grain. Beech makes the best pins, being less brittle than oak. The pin must be run up deep into both pieces.

19–20
Repairing the leg of a console with a pin.
The broken leg.
After repairing. The glue joint has been reinforced with a pin.

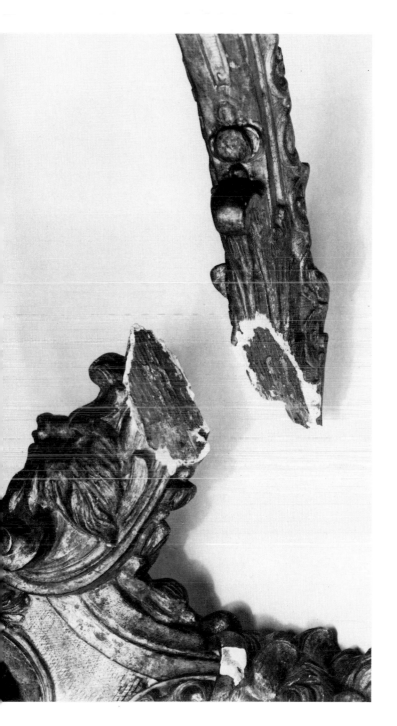

41

21
Fitting lime corner blocks inside the seat of a chair. They are as thick as the seat rails are wide. The holes left by the upholstery have been plugged with plastic wood.

Dowels can be purchased in the shops, but the restorer can also make his own pins to the exact size required by hammering a square length of wood through a toothed die. Dowel-pins need to be gone over with a toothing plane in any case.

INLAYS

The trouble with inlays is that they are irreversible and damage the carcase of the piece of furniture, which may be as beautiful as the outside. The most widely-used type of inlaid key is the *double dovetail* or 'butterfly', as it is sometimes called (fig. 8; ill. 17). The restorer brings the two elements togeth-er and cuts out a third of the thickness of the wood to insert the key, which should be of the same wood as the piece, or some hard wood (oak), and lie with its grain at right angles to the joint. The waist of the key needs to be fairly wide. Its shape makes it a useful strengthener but one that certain restorers consider inadequate.

Inlays may take other forms. For example, one can cut into the wood along the whole length of the joint and bed in a straight strengthening piece with its grain lying at right angles to the joint; or several pieces may be glued side by side.

STRENGTHENING PIECES
USED INSIDE

Strengthening pieces glued inside a piece of furniture qualify as reversible because they can be re-

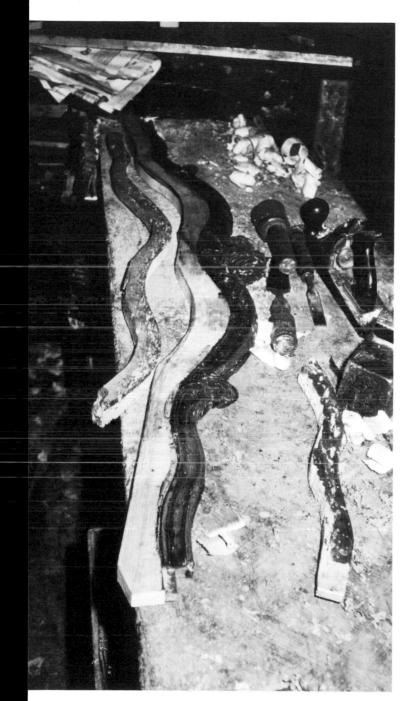

moved at any time. They are used when one does not want to cut into the piece, or it may be that the piece cannot be dismantled and one has no alternative. Inside a chest of drawers, for example (ill. 16), the restorer can add all the reinforcement he thinks necessary, although this is not the case when the piece is veneered internally. A disadvantage of this kind of strengthening is that the glue may lose its adhesive power.

Blocks (ill. 16) are used to hold the sides of a split together, stop a crack growing, or lock joints between uprights and cross-pieces. They are cut

24
The wood-carver's tool-kit. Left to right: maul, three gouges plus one that is almost flat, two firmers, two angle gouges, two double-angle gouges, two burins, two hatching gouges for doing ribs, three rifflers for finishing places that are awkward to get at.

25
The wood-carver's grinding-wheel, actually a series of small sandstone wheels of different breadths.

with the grain from soft-wood or the same type of wood as the piece of furniture concerned. When they are glued over a split it is with the grain at right angles to the line of fracture. Often when this is not completely straight it is better to fix a number of small blocks side by side rather than one big one. When he is unable to clamp them the restorer uses friction gluing, warming the block before applying the glue and fixing it in place.

26–7
Restoring a solid mahogany carved panel from an Empire piano. The missing portions are renewed on a symmetrical basis.

26 Fitting the new pieces of mahogany, which are glued flush to the panel before stripping.

Corner blocks (ill. 21) are a type of block designed to strengthen the joints between legs and seat rails at the corners of a chair-seat. Some restorers will have nothing to do with them, regarding them as unaesthetic and preferring to dismantle the chair and remake the tenons. In some cases, however, it is detrimental to remove the upholstery and dismantle. Other restorers, even when they have reglued the joints, add corner blocks as a matter of course for extra security and in order to counteract

45

27 Carving is completed on the renewed portions and the panel is stripped.

the strain to which the seat rails are subjected during re-upholstery as a result of all the tacks that have to be hammered in. Corner blocks are particularly useful when the seat rails are narrow and worm-eaten.

Corner blocks must be of lime or poplar, softwoods that glue well – not deal, for example – and they must be almost as thick as the seat rails are broad. Thin corner blocks of beech are no good at all. Generally the inside face is shaped to a concave line in the interests of elegance but also because this is more convenient for the purposes of sprung upholstery and means that the blocks can be screwed on if required. If the legs have not been reglued they are held still while the corner blocks are put in place. If the blocks are well glued it is not necessary to screw them; nevertheless some restorers do so, but not until the glue has dried. They must on no account be nailed.

New pieces

These must be of the same wood as the piece of furniture they are to strengthen – old wood if possible – and they must have their grain lying in the same direction. If they do not form part of a joint they can be glued with vinyl adhesive. Large pieces are mounted on the old portion by means of a tongue, tenon or pins; or they can be glued on flush, as was often the case with new pieces added to old carved furniture. In the case of solid-wood furniture they will be camouflaged at the staining stage.

SCARF GLUING

Scarf gluing is a process often used to join elements together. It consists in bringing the two elements together in the same plane and making an oblique joint between them. This involves trimming the old portion to present a slanting edge. The slant should be as great as possible in order to offer a large area for gluing and to bring the surface of contact as nearly as possible in line with the grain. This applies particularly when what is being added is the bottom

28
Overhauling the runners of a drawer. The bottom of the right-hand side of the drawer was worn down and a thickness has been glued on to bring it up to size.

of a leg or a piece of a seat rail. A scarf joint can be reinforced with a false tenon or a pin (fig. 9).

FALSE REBATE

The upholstery on chair-seats is nailed to a rebate running along the inside of the uprights and the back seat rail and the outside of the other seat rails. Seat rails and uprights often split at the rebate because of the nails or the traction of the webbing. If he wants to re-upholster the restorer must first make a new rebate by replacing the split portion; the upholstery will hide the new piece (fig. 10; ill. 23). All the split wood is chiselled away from the seat rail or upright, leaving only a thin remainder on the visible face (i.e. the outside on the back and the inside around the seat). A facing is all that is needed; in fact the thicker the piece added, the more solid the repair. The bare, straight surfaces are then rebate-planed. If the chair can be dismantled the new piece is fitted with a tenon at each end; otherwise it is glued. As a general rule – and particularly on a mahogany chair – the best wood to use for the new piece is beech, which grips upholstery nails well and has less tendency to split than other woods.[7]

CARVING

Adding material to a carved portion (ills. 26–7) involves cutting it out to roughly the section of the carving to be replaced but a bit thicker, to allow for taking some away. The piece is glued on and pressed, the motif to be copied is traced on to it, and the restorer carves it out. The carving must be done very carefully indeed, even if the piece of furniture is to be painted or gilded, because it may at some time in the future be stripped down to the bare wood.

Drawer slides

Drawers fit into an arrangement called a drawer slide that enables them to glide in and out. This consists of an upper runner, a lower runner, and a guide (fig. 11; ill. 28). These and the drawer eventually wear one another out of true. Overhauling drawer slides is one of the least evident yet most difficult and time-consuming of the restorer's tasks. The first step is to even off the top and bottom of the sides of the drawer and add a thickness underneath, and sometimes one on top as well. Worn runners are evened up in the same way. Then a groove or rebate is made in them and a further thickness glued in. A glued piece can also be added to the guides, or they can be unglued, straightened, and glued back on. If they need replacing, the new ones must be of a softer wood than the drawer; otherwise they will leave a groove.

VENEER

A piece of veneered furniture consists of a solid-wood carcase (usually of oak or deal) covered with a thin, glued facing of one or more types of wood different from that of the carcase – they may be indigenous or exotic – or quite other materials such as tortoise-shell, various metals, etc. Veneering made its first appearance in medieval Italy in the form of a mixed process known as *tarsia certosina* (ill. 51) in which motifs were cut with a chisel from wood anything up to 5 mm thick and inlaid in graves chiselled out of certain parts of a piece of solid-wood furniture. Eventually whole pieces were covered with juxtaposed elements. In the sixteenth century the technique began to spread to neighbouring countries. By the seventeenth century veneers had become thinner and motifs were cut out with a saw.

From the point of view of appearance there are three types of veneering: single-leaf veneering (ill. 34), matched patterns, in which pieces of veneer are used in geometrical arrangements (ill. 48), and marquetry work, in which individually cut motifs (flowers, objects, figures, etc.) stand out against a background of a different kind of wood (ill. 30).

In matched patterns and marquetry the pieces of veneer can be cut and glued one by one; more usually, though, the different components of a panel are cut out and assembled dry, marquetry motifs being inserted in the holes cut in the background to take them; a sheet of paper is then glued to the face side (the side that will eventually show), the panel is glued to the backing, and the paper is removed once the glue is dry.

Two variants of this process are possible in the case of marquetry. A technique introduced in the seventeenth century and used mainly on what is called Boulle marquetry makes it possible to cut out ground and decor simultaneously. Two different veneers (wood or any other material) in contrasting colours are placed one on top of the other; a template of the motif to be obtained is then placed on top and the motif cut out of both leaves at once with a very fine saw. When the leaves are separated, two decors and two backgrounds with matching outlines are left, each of which can be paired off with its opposite. Marquetry is referred to as *première partie* when a light-coloured decor figures in a darker ground (e.g. brass in tortoise-shell, in the

29
Inlaid marquetry. Drop front of the upper part and one of the two leaves of the lower part of the carcase of a Louis XVI wardrobe secretaire. The carcase had split in a number of places and the veneer has been removed (see also ills. 52 and 57). On a rosewood background marquetry flowers had been inlaid with a burin, as the traces on the carcase show.

case of Boulle marquetry) and as *contre-partie* when the reverse is the case. The method makes it possible to veneer two pieces of furniture in a single operation – or even three, if the same pattern is cut out of three different materials – but it has the disadvantage of leaving a tiny gap (kerf) between decorative motifs and background due to the passage of the saw-blade.

Another method, discussed by Roubo,[1] was used in eighteenth-century France, particularly on curved Louis XV furniture.[2] This consisted in first gluing the background to the groundwork, cutting out the motifs one by one, tracing round them on the background with a pointed knife, removing the unwanted pieces of background material with a burin, and inlaying the motifs (ill. 29).

In the Netherlands and in Italy marquetry was at certain periods assembled and glued face side up to a sheet of paper that was then glued to the groundwork and left there – with the risk of its subsequently disintegrating.

Being dry, thin, and held in place with glue, a wood veneer is in principle stable and should behave as if it were one with the groundwork (though of course this is not true of thick veneers such as those used on mid-seventeenth-century French ebony cabinets, for example). But the wood it is glued to has different properties than it has itself, and cabinet-makers in the past did not take our modern precaution of veneering both sides of the groundwork. Consequently under certain circumstances veneer and groundwork will not react in the same way, and the resultant tension between them may cause the veneer to lift. In too humid an atmosphere it will buckle, and when a period of humidity abruptly gives way to a hot spell it will shrink and crack in thin parallel splits along the grain; if the grain happens to follow that of the groundwork it will do so even more readily.

But most of the damage to veneered furniture comes from play in the groundwork and from the glue.

30
Top of a Louis XIV commode. One of the joints of the carcase has given and torn the marquetry right along the split (Paris, Cluny Museum).

31
Veneer that has lifted in bubbles.

The groundwork, for example, may shrink and split, or the joints, which do not necessarily coincide with those of the veneer, may open up (ill. 30). These movements of the groundwork begin by making their presence felt under the veneer and end by actually tearing and lifting it along the places where accidents have occurred, no matter how well it has been glued.

Glue that has been inadequately pressed out forms a layer between veneer and groundwork that crystallizes and prevents the two from adhering. It also becomes dehydrated when exposed to heat. All adhesion lost, the veneer starts to lift at the joints or in bubbles, which may sometimes be invisible (ill. 31).

All these accidents may, if not treated, mean that bits of veneer come away and are lost.

A necessary prelude to repairing veneered work is to consolidate the groundwork, i.e. the carcase of the piece of furniture, checking the condition of the wood, joints, legs, rails, drawer slides, and so on. It is no good repairing the veneer on a drawer only to have it ripped off again because the drawer is not functioning properly. Restoring a carcase often involves ungluing and removing the veneer.

Ungluing veneer

Whether stripping is done after or before ungluing depends on the piece of furniture being treated. If this is in very bad shape it is best to begin by stripping, mainly because this will show up any patching done during previous restorations and because in cases where one is not sure about a wood that needs patching now it may assist identification. Often,

however, restorers will prefer to strip after regluing. There is always a danger of stripper getting under the veneer, and if it does so all trace of it must be painstakingly removed before regluing, otherwise the glue will not take. Furthermore when veneer is stripped first there is a risk of parts that have lifted escaping notice at the regluing stage and moving subsequently when they are subjected to moisture at the staining and varnishing stages.

There is no harm in stressing once again the importance of keeping any ungluing to a minimum. Veneer should only be lifted, whether locally or completely, when the groundwork underneath it needs repairing or when there is no glue left to hold it on. It should be possible to feel whether the glue is still good. What is the point of removing everything if it is? On the other hand the restorer has to remove bits of veneer with holes in them or too obviously poorly fitting pieces dating from previous restorations. Even these, however, will be left on surfaces that do not show too much or where they are hidden by mounts, except when they occur in cross-cut or rotary-cut veneer.

It is as well to be clear about the risks involved in ungluing veneer, particularly that of breaking certain woods (snake wood, mahogany curl, burrs, cross-cuts, plane, sycamore) that will be hard to replace in the same nuances as they have on the piece of furniture or even impossible to replace at all. Tiny bits of marquetry – flower stems, for example – may easily get lost if unglued. Old, hand-

32
Ungluing a mahogany veneer panel. After reheating the glue with a veneering iron the restorer lifts the veneer with a steel blade.

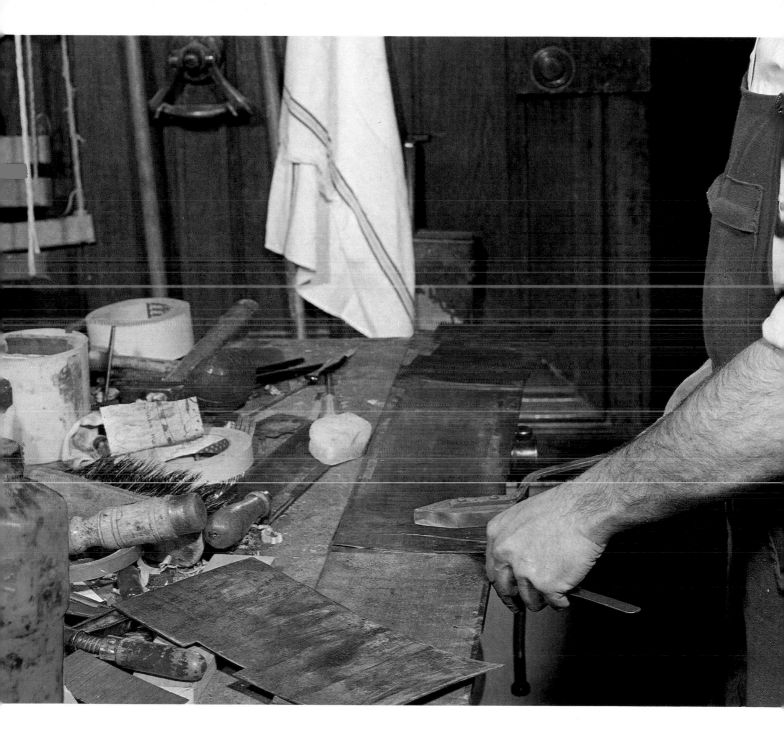

sawn veneers and particularly inlaid marquetry (see p. 50) both present special problems, and finally there is the danger, at the regluing stage, of not getting the veneer back in exactly the right place, particularly on a curved groundwork. In fact in borderline cases this may be the deciding factor: removing the veneer from a flat surface involves slightly less risk than removing it from a curved surface.

Veneer is removed either dry or by one of several processes involving moisture. A variety of methods may be necessary on any one piece of furniture if some parts unglue more easily than others. A very thin steel blade – blunt, to avoid piercing the veneer – is used for lifting. The dry method is preferable, and if the glue has lost its grip one will need only to slide the blade under the veneer and lift it off. If it resists the restorer warms it with a veneering iron to soften or burn it, taking care to place a sheet of heavy paper or card between iron and veneer in order not to burn the wood (ill. 32).

If necessary a piece of furniture that is to be completely deveneered can be left in a damp cellar for two or three days to assist the process, which will then need to be carried out immediately; to avoid any risk the veneer, once removed, must be placed in a press, and the restorer will wait until the carcase is thoroughly dry before beginning restoration.

If the glue still resists after heating, the restorer uses a syringe to inject 95° surgical spirit under the veneer (ill. 53).

In some cases none of these methods will work, however, and the restorer will have to use the steam process, a tricky operation that carries with it the risk of the veneer buckling, swelling, and refusing to fit back into place afterwards. The veneer is moistened with a damp cloth on which the restorer places a medium-hot iron (ill. 54). While lifting one section he moves the damping cloth and the iron on to the next. A way of speeding up the process is to cover the surface to be unglued the day before with a layer of moistened fine white sawdust.

Pieces of veneer that one does not wish to reglue can be burned away with the iron or removed with hammer and chisel. If he is removing a whole section of marquetry the restorer will tape the motifs together as he removes them, partly in order not to lose them and partly to make sure he gets them back in the same place (ill. 33). If a lot of the marquetry is missing this is a tricky operation, and the restorer will be well advised to leave the surround until last as this will give him something to go by.

When removing curved veneer that cannot be worked flat, it is a good idea to start by making a caul to fit the shape of the curve (see below, pp. 63–4). As he removes the veneer the restorer lays it on the caul upside down and fixes it there to keep its shape; the caul can subsequently be used to make new pieces, scrape the back of the veneer, level it off in the case of Boulle marquetry (see p. 89), and press it down at the regluing stage.[3]

It is easier to remove veneer from oak than from soft-wood groundwork, soft-woods offering better adhesion. In the case of deal carcases the top layer of fibres sometimes comes away on the back of the veneer. Rosewood, violet wood and purple wood unglue fairly easily – unlike mahogany, for example. Some woods, as I have said, are rather fragile when removed, and if the restorer needs to unglue any burrs, curls, or stained sycamores, for example, he will dry them in a press to stop them buckling.

Any old glue is removed from the groundwork and the back of the veneer with a toothing plane. The

next stage is to carry out such repairs to the carcase as may be necessary.

Replacements

One obvious rule that follows from what I have been saying about ungluing is this: as little replacing as possible should be done where the old veneer still holds, not only in order to comply with the general principle of retaining a maximum of original elements but also because it is often difficult to find exactly the right wood for replacements; and even supposing one has the right wood, the grain, figure and colour may not be the same.

This is why, for example, when a piece of veneer has been thinned down too much by previous restora-

33
Reconstructing veneer. The veneer has been removed from the two leaves of the secretaire in ill. 29 and is held together by strips of adhesive tape applied to the front face. Left, the left-hand leaf (verso); right, the right-hand leaf (see also ill. 45).

tions, it is not replaced but instead brought up to thickness. The worn veneer is removed, a thin packing piece (e.g. of walnut veneer) is glued to the back of it, and the two together are reglued to the groundwork, leaving the outward appearance of the piece unchanged. Similarly it is sometimes better to treat small perforations and blemishes not by replacing material but by touching them up with shellac varnish, even though this often means that they will eventually show up again.

Where, however, the original veneer has actually disappeared, or is so frayed and split as to have become unusable, or has been poorly matched in

55

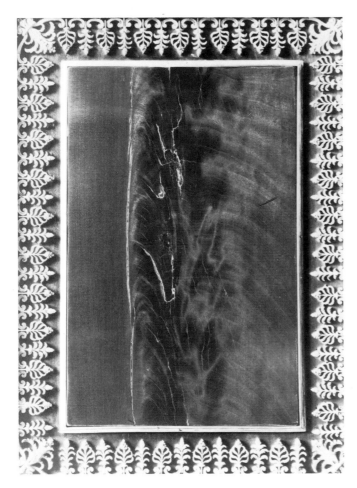

34
Badly restored veneer. The left-hand portion of this panel of moiré mahogany veneer has been replaced with straight-grained mahogany.

it is better, as I have said, to use old veneer rather than try and stain new wood to match. It may even be possible, where only small patches are required, to re-use damaged material from the same piece of furniture. Or sometimes the restorer will repair the visible surfaces of a piece with material taken from less visible parts; this is a risky solution, however, and should be used only in emergencies. Where the replacement veneer is thicker than the original, levelling it off after regluing would remove the surface colour; it is better to glue the replacement face down on a sheet of paper and scrape the excess thickness off the back. If he has to use new veneer the restorer will first smooth off a small area and dampen or varnish it to find out what its colour will be like after finishing.

Replacements, whether of missing material or of damaged material, generally speaking fall into two categories. Ideally the shape of the place to be filled or the piece of veneer to be replaced is already defined. It may be an element in a marquetry design, or it may lie neatly in the grain of the wood; a damaged knot, for example, is removed and replaced with another knot, the two operations being performed with the aid of a pinking iron.

But supposing conditions are less than ideal – what is the best shape to give a patch in order to make it merge with the grain? Repairs across the grain show up more, and one tends to avoid them wherever possible (fig. 12). It is satisfactory to have a patch run up to an edge or joint, and where the missing or damaged area is at or near an edge the restorer will use a tapering patch to butt against it. Where the replacement area is in the centre of a surface he will use a strip running the whole width of the veneer, always supposing he has the wood available and the

previous restorations, the restorer will of course have to replace it.

The wood selected for replacements should be as nearly as possible of the same type, figure and colour as the original (ill. 34), though the type may be difficult or even – in the case of tiny marquetry elements, for example – impossible to identify.[4] And area involved is not too enormous (though in fact a narrow replacement strip often shows up more than a broad one). Where this cannot be done or where it would remove too much veneer, the restorer uses a diamond-shaped patch that will 'disappear' in the grain. If the grain in the place concerned is wavy or curly, a patch with a corresponding shape will disappear more easily. As little sound veneer should be removed as possible. Rather than break it the restorer will often prefer to settle for a visible patch. The patch once selected, it can sometimes be fitted directly in the hole with the aid of a chisel. More usually, though, the restorer takes an impression of the place to be filled by laying a sheet of white paper over it and rubbing the edge of the hole with a pencil. Another method is to lay a sheet of carbon paper on top of the first sheet and a second sheet on top of the carbon to stop it tearing, which again produces an impression on the first sheet. The pattern is then glued to the veneer, and once the glue is dry the patch is cut out and glued to the groundwork. Afterwards the paper is removed with a warm veneering iron or a damp sponge.

Patches with straight edges are cut either with a veneering saw or with a chisel (ill. 36). Sawing is more difficult when it comes to a marquetry element with a wavy outline. The professional inlayer still uses the traditional sawing horse consisting of a bench and a vice (ill. 11). Sitting astride the bench with the vertical vice in front of him, he uses his free hand to hold and move the veneer in the vice, which is foot-operated with the aid of a cord. In the eighteenth century inlayers sawed horizontally, using a marquetry saw or fret-saw fitted with the appropriate blade, this depending on the material to be cut (ill. 36). The nineteenth century introduced an

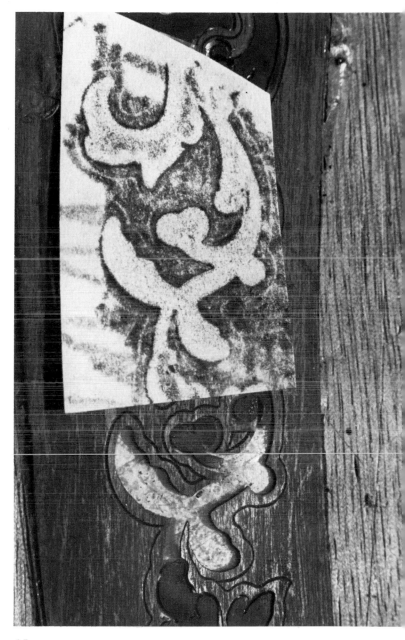

35
Taking an impression of a missing tortoise-shell marquetry motif.

improvement by mounting on the right of the vice an arm taking a travelling saw frame that was operated by hand and that also moved horizontally and at right angles to the vice. These sawing horses are no longer manufactured nowadays, having been replaced by the electric jigsaw (the blade of which also moves vertically). Both sawing horse and jigsaw can be used to cut the same shape out of several leaves of veneer simultaneously, but they can only do vertical edges. The blades, which are of course extremely thin, are often manufactured by inlayers themselves out of pieces of watch spring.[5]

But this kind of equipment takes up a lot of room and besides is hardly justifiable economically for the restorer; he tends to stick to the marquetry saw, but uses it in the vertical plane. He holds the veneer with his free hand, possibly between two blocks of wood – in which case a sheet of sandpaper placed under the veneer will stop it slipping. With a marquetry saw one can also do bevel sawing, which is essential when replacing inlaid marquetry elements, the edges of marquetry motifs being bevelled inwards and those of the background outwards. A bevelled edge can also be achieved with a gouge. Where the restorer has to replace a large area that includes a piece of inlaid marquetry work, he will veneer the background first and cut out of this the graves for the motifs. Finally, certain brittle veneers such as cross-cut violet wood are glued to a sheet of paper before they are sawn.

Once the patch is cut out it will need to be trimmed before gluing. A well-trimmed patch will be invisible. The edges are levelled off with chisel or metal plane.

Marquetry may be shaded or incised, and if the restorer has sufficient information to go on he can reconstitute this decoration. But sometimes one has only the outline of the missing motif and knows nothing of how it was decorated. Shading is done with very fine sand laid to a depth of several centimetres in a metal container. This is heated to a high temperature on a gas stove. After making tests, the restorer plunges the patch or part of the patch into the sand. The temperature and the period of immersion will depend on the type of wood concerned and the shade required. If the temperature is not the same right through the sand the result will be a graduated tint.

The restoration of incised work is done at a later stage. On marquetry decorated with identical or symmetrical incised motifs, the restorer takes a tracing of a well-preserved motif before rubbing down and transfers it to the worn or new motifs during finishing.

The replacement of strings – those thin strips that sometimes frame veneer panels – poses special problems.[6] Composite strings are made up first before being glued to the groundwork. The restorer nails a batten to a board, lays his first string (which may consist of several pieces laid end to end) up against it, applies glue to the visible edge, lays his second string against the first, and nails another batten in position to hold the two strings pressed together. Once the glue has dried the restorer adds the third string by the same method, and so on as required. In some cases it may be a good idea to glue the strings to a piece of paper as well.

I mentioned shellac as a useful alternative to replacing veneer that is only slightly holed. Shellac has been used to touch up veneer since the eighteenth century, as we know from Roubo: 'The method by which a mixture of shellac, rosin or other ingre-

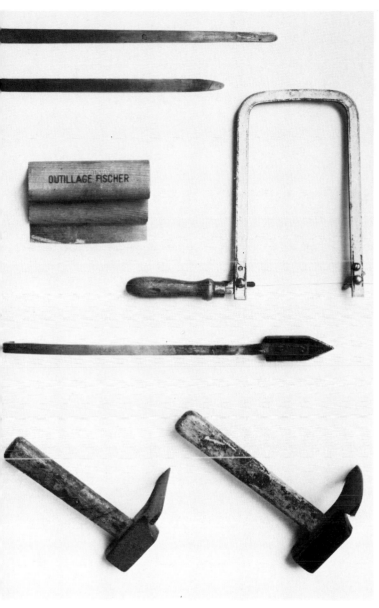

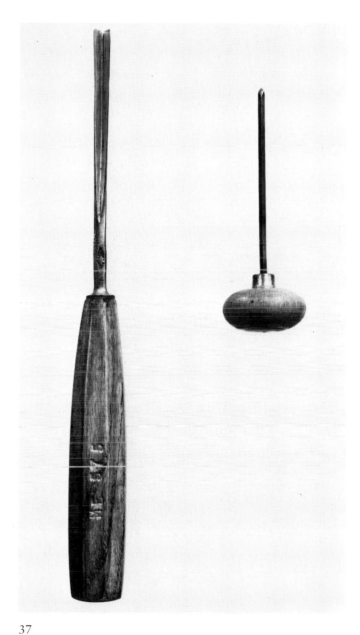

36
Some of the tools used in restoring veneer. Left to right: steel blades, veneering saw, marquetry saw (fret-saw), veneering iron, veneering hammers (one convex, for concave surfaces; the other straight).

37
Burins. Left, hollow burin used for engraving wood. Right, copperplate engraver's burin used in the restoration of Boulle marquetry.

dients with wax is used to polish veneer undoubtedly has much to recommend it; it is also, however, much used to disguise faults of workmanship, particularly in the eyes of those whose knowledge of such matters is less than complete.'[7] Stick shellac is not recommended; it is better to use flake shellac, which the restorer can tint himself with various earths. Using a hot iron – and taking care not to scorch the wood – the restorer melts the shellac and applies it to the hole. Once it has set, he removes any excess and can proceed immediately to rub down. Over-obtrusive 'shellackings' can be disguised at the varnishing stage.

Regluing veneer

Whichever gluing method is adopted, certain principles always obtain. If the groundwork and the back of the veneer are bare, one 'makes room' for the glue by marking them with a toothing plane, even where this has been done already, in order to give the glue a better purchase. Some people apply glue only to the groundwork, but this is wrong; it needs to be applied to both surfaces. Finally, when pressing it is important to start from the centre of the area being glued in order to drive the glue out towards the edges and expel any surplus; where one is sliding glue under the veneer without removing the latter, one starts pressing at the point farthest away from the edge.

It is only possible to glue two surfaces that are in perfect contact. If the veneer has buckled and become stiff and dry, it must first be straightened. Slight undulation may be removed by simply ironing it out with a veneering iron (see below). If the

buckle is more marked, however, there is a danger of cracking the veneer, and the correct treatment is to unglue the panel, moisten one or both sides of the veneer, possibly glue it lightly to a sheet of paper, and then place it under a warm zinc caul; the glue stiffens it as it dries out under the caul.

REGLUING WITH A VENEERING HAMMER, PIECE BY PIECE

This is a difficult method (ill. 36), but because it avoids the necessity for removing the veneer completely when the groundwork is in good condition it is an excellent way to restore veneered furniture. Using a glue that grips immediately, the restorer can reglue damaged veneer bit by bit as he investigates it.

He works with the piece of furniture between him and the light, which if it grazes the surface being examined will show up the places that need regluing. These are not always obvious, and one must explore the surface not only with one's eyes but also by touch, by sound,[8] and with the point of a blade in order to find out whether the veneer has come away or is about to do so. The eye alone may be deceived in the case of an apparently level surface, and the wise restorer will take other opinions, as it were. In fact the veneer may be just hanging on and if not treated would come away during subsequent operations involving moisture. Bubbles are more difficult to detect in veneer that has been rubbed down too much and is very thin.

Where the veneer is not actually split, some restorers iron any bubbles flat without bothering to introduce fresh glue. It is, however, absolutely essential to do so. The method is to run a strong thin blade in the direction of the grain and make a cut along the whole length of the bubble. If an edge has already come unglued this is lifted (after carefully strengthening it with adhesive tape if it is beginning to fray). Glue is then introduced – plentifully, to ensure that it will spread throughout the affected area – with a softer steel blade, e.g. from a corset. Where the veneer has come away completely the glue is brushed on.

The restorer then takes a moderately damp sponge in one hand and a veneering iron[9] in the other. With the sponge he wipes the area beneath which he has just applied glue; by moistening the wood this will stop the iron burning it and allow the iron to glide better. The iron, which must be warm and applied with some pressure, warms the setting glue, spreads it into all the places it was impossible to reach directly, and, by reheating any original glue that has not perished, amalgamates the two adhesives. Thin or brittle veneer is warmed gradually with the iron, otherwise the iron may pull at it.

Pressing very hard this time, the restorer goes over the area again with the cross-peen of his veneering hammer, which makes the glue grip and expels any surplus (this is essential, otherwise it will form a thickness beneath the veneer). The excess glue is them removed with a sponge. Both iron and hammer press and level simultaneously. Such mingling of old and new glues as may take place under the veneer ensures that the still sound original veneer and the reglued portions adhere firmly to one another.

Occasionally the hammer may appear inadequate when it comes to fixing certain elements, particularly on curves, in which case it is as well to place a small thin wooden caul (of Gaboon multi-ply, for example) on top of the piece of reglued veneer, holding it there with a hand cramp or with the aid of veneering pins driven into a crack or a joint.

As he reglues piece by piece in this way the restorer will also carry out any repairs that may be necessary to the groundwork, applying plastic wood to worm-eaten portions, trimming joints, etc. And any new pieces he will cut out and fit one by one, moulding them round curved areas by heating them with the iron but without too much moisture.

Hammer regluing is recommended for curved surfaces and particularly for inlaid marquetry, where to unglue the whole thing is dangerous (see p. 50). The pieces to be fixed are at the same time replaced in exactly their original position and immediately levelled. There is no need to take any risks, for example when one does not know whether a piece of marquetry is inlaid or not. The hammer method can also be used where veneer has been removed completely, particularly if it is a question of a small area, whether flat or curved.

CAUL VENEERING

Depending on the shape and size of the surface to be reglued and on whether the restorer has been able to dismantle the veneered panel or not, he has recourse to other methods. All these make use of cauls of one sort or another through which the pressure of cramps or other tools is transferred to the veneer.

Where an entire panel has been removed, glue is first brushed on to both surfaces, the veneer is fitted into place on the groundwork, and if the panel is flat it can be provisionally held down with weights. The veneer is then anchored by fixing it to the groundwork with adhesive tape. If this is not possible the restorer drives very thin veneering pins (as few as possible) into the joints, along the outer

edge of the panel, or where the mounts come. The pins are greased, and enough is left showing to allow them to be extracted easily afterwards. The surface of the veneer is then covered with a sheet of cardboard into which the pins will sink. The next step is to position the caul or cauls.

Cauls

The object of the caul is to achieve a perfectly flat and even surface and also, because it is used hot, to warm the glue as the veneer is pressed. A caul needs to be heated uniformly to exactly the right temperature. If it is too hot it may burn the glue; if it is not hot enough it will not serve its purpose. A sheet of paper (preferably newspaper) is always placed between it and the wood to prevent caul and veneer from sticking, should glue ooze out of the joints. The type of caul used will depend on whether the surface is flat or curved.

Flat surfaces

The usual sort of caul is a sheet of zinc or aluminium between 3 and 4 mm thick, which is heated without burning it (i.e. below 100 °C). If the thickness of the veneer is not uniform, however, a sheet of cardboard of the appropriate hardness and gauge is used with the object of hugging the surface and distributing the pressure more evenly. This metal or

38
Sand veneering. The concave back of this Boulle marquetry console (see also ill. 58) is veneered with copper leaf. This is reglued by pressing it between a shaped caul and a sandbag with a wooden caul on top.

39
Shaped cauls and counter-cauls for veneering Boulle marquetry, some with an intermediate cardboard caul.

40
Veneering a table leg with a shaped caul made up of several thicknesses of plywood. Nailed to the caul are bearers for the hand cramps to impinge on.

cardboard caul is covered with a 20–22 mm thick hardwood caul.

Curved surfaces

The traditional method here is sand veneering (ill. 38). A quantity of very fine sand in a canvas bag very slightly larger than the area to be glued is warmed in a container. The sandbag is placed on top of the glued panel, moulded to its shape, and covered with one or more wooden cauls. It is a tricky process; the veneer must be anchored very precisely, for it would be disastrous if it were to slip during pressing or otherwise fail to find its exact original position.

If the curve is not very pronounced it is possible to use a zinc or cardboard caul here too, or a piece of flexible plywood with bearers nailed to it. For pronounced curves a specially shaped caul will have to be made – often of solid wood (ill. 39) or several thicknesses of plywood (ill. 40), or it may be of battens laid side by side and glued. If the place is curved in both directions it is best to take a plaster or synthetic resin impression of it, after first carefully insulating the surface. Where plaster is used the restorer simply builds a wooden box round the area and pours the plaster in, reinforcing it with tow, wire or other materials (ill. 41–3). Where synthetic resin is used, the area is framed with modelling clay and the liquid resin poured in together with its hardener. Sometimes a thin cardboard caul is placed between the veneer and the shaped caul,

63

41–3
Using plaster to make a shaped caul for a piece of Boulle marquetry:
1 The element to be unglued, which is curved in both directions.
2 The marquetry having been removed, shuttering is erected to take the plaster.
3 The plaster cast and the reconstructed veneer.

provided that this does not modify the curve. It may be complemented with a counter-caul (ill. 39).

Pressing
Depending on the size of the area to be glued, the restorer may use hand cramps or veneering frames. The important point is to ensure that pressure is exerted uniformly in order to avoid trapping thicknesses of glue.

Hand presses may be of wood or metal and impinge on the caul covering the veneer panel; spot regluing may require only one, while larger areas will need several distributed over the surface of the caul.

Where the panel is a large one and the restorer has been able to dismantle it, he will press the reglued veneer with veneering frames (ill. 44). These are rectangular wooden or metal frames consisting of two uprights and two cross-pieces, the upper cross-piece taking a number of large screws. They are used side by side, parallel with one another. A heavy caul is placed across the lower cross-pieces. On top of this comes the surface to be reglued, covered with its cauls, and lastly a pressing caul is placed on top for the screws to impinge on. These are tightened slowly, one after another, beginning in the middle, moving outwards to the others, then coming back to the middle, and so on.

Whichever method of pressing he is using, the restorer always stops at one point to check whether the glue has been properly evacuated and then presses again. It is best to allow the glue as long as possible to dry, leaving the work in the press for between 12 and 24 hours.

STRAP VENEERING

This is used on cylindrical members such as columns or legs. Glue is applied to the groundwork only. The veneer is moistened outside or inside to enable it to assume the required curve; it is then placed in position and held there by means of pins driven into the joints. The next step is to wind a strap round the veneered surface and fix the ends of this, again with pins. The whole bundle is then moistened and afterwards exposed to an even heat all round. The combined action of heat and steam re-warms the glue as the strap shrinks and presses the veneer tightly against the groundwork. The heat

44
Veneering frames.

is removed just before the strap dries out, otherwise it would burn. The strap is left on for another few hours to give the glue time to dry; it is then unwound.

Having completed the regluing process (ill. 45) the restorer removes any pins he may have used. A damp sponge, spatula or warm iron will get rid of any excess glue, the paper placed under the caul, and any adhesive tape used to strengthen the veneer during regluing.

If any new pieces have been added and they overlap the groundwork, they will need to be trimmed. This is done first with a saw and then with a chisel or special spokeshave (ill. 13).

One fairly serious consequence is that the hot cauls used will remove any varnish, meaning that the

45
The secretaire of ill. 29 with the veneer reglued.

piece of furniture will have to be revarnished. In cases of very localized damage, however, on a piece of furniture that is otherwise in good condition, it is possible to reglue without affecting the varnish, provided that one can lift the unglued veneer – for example at the edge of the piece – and introduce the glue underneath. The glue must be used very hot and the veneer pressed down with a warm caul.

Tarsia certosina

One or two remarks are called for in connection with restoring this special type of decoration. As with other kinds of marquetry, the first step is to check whether the pieces still hold or not. Being let into graves in the actual groundwork, they usually adhere well. But they will frequently have been attacked by woodworm, particularly since they are often cut from pear wood. The surface, where wax has preserved it, may appear to be in good condition while under the surface the wood is all eaten away. It may be necessary to unglue and reglue each piece in turn, filling in any cavities.

If elements are missing and the restorer has enough clues with which to 'reconstruct' them, he first scrapes off any fibres that may have remained stuck to the groundwork before putting the new pieces in place. In the absence of adequate information, he must leave such lacunae as they are. The effect will not be too disturbing since the wood showing through will be of the same kind as the surround; it may be slightly lighter than the surround in colour because of its former protective covering, but it can be retouched to make it less obvious.

Tarsia certosina is often decorated with broad, deep incisions filled with very dark tinted wax, which is applied with a spatula.

FINISHING VARNISHED AND WAXED FURNITURE

One cannot over-emphasize either the length or the importance of the operations known collectively as finishing. Poorly performed, they can completely cancel out an otherwise good piece of restoration. Finishing may comprise up to four stages: stripping, rubbing down, staining and, as the case may be, varnishing, wax filling or wax polishing.

Stripping

The purpose of this is to remove varnish or wax and re-expose the natural colour of the wood. As far as veneered furniture is concerned, it is not always necessary to use a chemical stripper since the iron or hot cauls used for regluing will probably have got rid of most of the varnish or wax and rubbing down will remove the rest. Dry stripping is in fact the best method. Where a chemical stripper is needed to dissolve the varnish, the restorer cannot of course use a product based on potassium, caustic soda or ammonia, all of which stain wood and require rinsing. He will need something volatile. There are various fairly gentle solvents on the market, notably containing acetone and paraffin, which do not attack wood or affect its colour, except where this derives from a stain (which they will of course eliminate). Stripper is applied with a broad, flat brush in two coats to make it bite well. Depending on the circumstances, stripper and dissolved varnish can be removed with a spatula or by rubbing with steel wool in the direction of the grain. They will tend to collect in the corners, and great care may be needed to remove them completely. If necessary the operation is repeated with fresh applications of stripper. Wax can be got rid of with the aid of the same products or with benzine or white spirit. Turpentine also dilutes it but may soil and darken the wood.

Rubbing down

The object of rubbing down (ill. 46) is to produce a smooth surface by removing any defects (as far as this can be done without risk) and to recover up to a point the original colour of the wood. One of the restorer's most stringent rules must be to rub down as little as possible. The operation, which should affect only the surface, must be performed with the most extreme care. Rubbing down too vigorously will soon remove the patinated colour from a piece of wood. Some restorers still make the mistake of

46
Rubbing down. Left to right: scraper, steel (for sharpening scraper), rubbing-down block consisting of a piece of wood with a cork sole a few millimetres thick glued underneath it.

taking the whole surface off with a scraper[1] in order to obtain a fresher colour, an approach that is particularly catastrophic when applied to veneered furniture, which has often been rubbed down to the limit anyway by previous restorers. Scraping, by reducing the thickness of veneer, increases the risk of the next restorer perforating it. If the worst comes to the worst, it is better to leave a bump than try and remove it at all costs.

There is a place for the scraper, however, and that is for levelling off replacement pieces on solid-wood furniture and removing mechanical saw marks from veneered furniture.

When rubbing down, cabinet-makers and restorers use progressively finer gauges of glass-paper wrapped round a cork block. For getting into recesses and for finishing off, the glass-paper is held in the fingers. Rubbing down is done in the direction of the grain, except in the case of curls or burrs, which are rubbed down with a circular motion. Turned members can be rubbed down with glass-paper by mounting them on a lathe.

For perfect rubbing down, particularly on porous woods, a useful trick is to wipe the surface with a sponge moistened with very hot water (removing the moisture immediately on veneer). As it dries, the surface roughens up, and it is then smoothed off again with very fine glass-paper. It is during the rubbing-down process, as I have already mentioned, that any incised work (ill. 37) is restored.

The surface of the wood is now flat but very dull in appearance. The next stage is to stain it if necessary, and finally it will be polished with wax or varnish.

If the piece is to be varnished, some restorers follow up the rubbing-down process by wiping the surface with a rag dipped in linseed-oil or vaseline. They do this for two reasons, claiming on the one hand that it revives the colour of the wood and on the other hand that, by making the polishing pad slide more easily, it speeds up the varnishing stage. Others condemn the practice, advancing different arguments. They say it makes filling (see p. 74) – always a difficult process on greasy woods such as Brazilian rosewood – altogether impossible, and that it prevents the wax stoppings that can be made at the filling stage from adhering; they also claim that the oil may subsequently reappear and impair the varnish. If in the case of a badly faded piece one does want to rub it with oil, it is absolutely essential to leave the piece to dry for a very long time – three weeks to a month – and to wipe it before filling.

Staining

The business of staining offers restorers scope for genuinely creative experimentation. Everyone has his own methods, but it is important not to 'go overboard'. Again the golden rule is to interfere as little as possible with the colour of the wood – a rule we have observed so far by using few replacement pieces, selecting them from old wood wherever possible, and keeping rubbing down to a minimum. These operations have already given us a certain colour: regluing, in the case of veneered furniture, stripping, and rubbing down have restored the wood more nearly to its true colour. Nevertheless for a variety of reasons it may be necessary to do some staining. If new wood has been used for replacement pieces, its colour will be too fresh. Old wood should as a rule not be stained, but if it has been rubbed down too vigorously in places, those places may be too bright. If on the other hand it is very faded, or if one part of a piece of furniture has lost more colour than the rest, the restorer may sometimes try to achieve a better overall tone.

In other words one is concerned to harmonize the piece as a whole by giving any new wood the colour it would have taken on with age and by restoring to old wood where necessary the colour it had before it was rubbed down. On the other hand, where a piece of furniture is made of several different woods, one wants to try and restore the original contrasts between them, which age will often have toned down by bringing the colours closer together; violet wood, for example, ends up looking like rosewood. Even so, I want to repeat that the role of staining must be kept to a minimum.

Staining calls for a wide knowledge of the way the colour of each type of wood evolves as it takes on patina. Even a well-stained piece will show up if the colour has been improperly reconstituted, although it is preferable to let it show than to use a process that involves a risk to the wood. Everything to do with staining in fact calls for enormous care. Tests must be carried out on the less visible parts of the piece. Even this is not recommended when the restorer is using acid stains, which he will try out on a separate piece of the same kind of wood, although the effect may occasionally be different on the piece of furniture (e.g. the same type of wood will give different colours depending on whether it is used solid or as veneer). Of exotic woods, Brazilian rose-wood and violet wood fade well; king-wood and snake-wood are more difficult to treat. Where one is staining new portions and old portions simultaneously, one uses the same product in different strengths. In some cases it is necessary to bleach a piece of wood before staining it. Correct staining is a matter of skill and experience; there is no universally valid rule for staining a particular type of wood, since each type exists in several variants. All we can do here is look quickly at the principal products used, which react differently on different woods and can be divided into two groups: those that are harmless to wood and those that are dangerous.

Water stains, which are sponged on generously and sponged off before they dry, can be used without risk. They serve principally to bring up the colour of indigenous woods left in their natural state – oak, beech, walnut, chestnut, fruit-tree woods – or to restore their patina. They are usually made from Cassel extract, tea or chicory. Cassel extract, which has replaced the traditional walnut stain for darkening wood, comes in powdered form; it is dissolved in water with the addition of a little alkali to serve as a mordant and possibly a dash of 'red mahogany', a dye that must be used very sparingly because it produces very bright colours. Tea leaves or powdered chicory are boiled in water and the liquor is best used warm. Alkanet root, applied as a decoction in turpentine to colour wax polish, is hardly ever used nowadays.

Of the second group, acid stains are particularly dangerous. Used to excess, they will corrode the glue in the joints of veneered work; they also darken wood, eventually scorching it irreparably. Great care must be taken not to apply acid stain beyond the area to be treated or to protect adjacent areas with paraffin. King-wood in particular needs to be protected from acids because if exposed even to the fumes it will take on a purply violet colour that is difficult to get rid of. Incidentally it is best to wear gloves when using certain acid stains.

Acids come in two forms: liquid, e.g. nitric and hydrochloric acid, which must be kept hermetically sealed and diluted before use with varying proportions of water, and crystalline; the latter are dissolved in hot water and can be used warm, examples being picric acid, to be used sparingly, and oxalic acid or salts of sorrel, very widely used particularly for bleaching but sometimes also for modifying or reviving a colour.

Acids are applied with a piece of cotton wound round a stick to form a brush (a real brush would of course be attacked by the acid). Once applied, the stain is rinsed lightly with a sponge dipped in warm water to prevent it from attacking the glue. When two acids are being used on the same spot, one to kill the colour and one to revive it, careful rinsing and drying are necessary between the two applications.

Alkali (ammonia), diluted with water or mixed with other products, also ages oak and chestnut. Again, great care is required because it can turn certain woods black, grey or red.

Thirty per cent hydrogen peroxide solution is used purely for bleaching wood. It is dangerous to use it on veneer because it may corrode the glue.

One of the most widely used products is bichromate of potash. This used to be available as crystals but now comes in the form of a yellow powder, to be dissolved in a greater or lesser quantity of water depending on the shade required. Bichromate of potash does not stain in its own right but by oxidizing the tannin in wood. It has the advantage of not attacking glue. It is used above all for darkening oak and mahogany. The latter is fairly light in colour when first converted but darkens with exposure to air; bichromate of potash brings out the whole gamut of shades. It has the effect of turning rosewood yellow. Other colorants can be added to it. The method of application is to sponge it on quickly and sponge off any surplus before it dries, because if a fresh application of bichromate is made to an area that has already dried it will darken the wood further and give a blotchy result.

Other products used are potassium and iron pyrolignite, which comes in liquid form. For touching up or restoring the colour of a piece of furniture made of ebonized wood, aniline black is used, a liquid product to which the restorer adds a mordant (alum or pyrogallic acid); the effect can be heightened at a later stage by colouring the varnish with black fuscin.

There is in fact a further possibility of recapturing certain shades and that is by very lightly tinting the varnish or wax with fuscins, powder colours derived from aniline (which is itself obtained by distilling tar). Spirit fuscins dissolve in spirit, oily fuscins in turpentine.

The finishing process can be continued as soon as the stain is dry, except where the wood has been treated with acids or similar products, in which case the piece of furniture must be left for between a fortnight and a month to give these time to complete their work; otherwise they will impair the varnish.

The piece of furniture must now be given a protec-

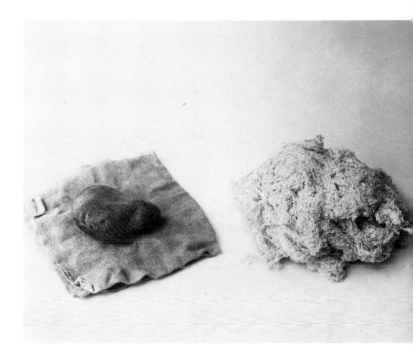

47
French polishing. Left, polishing pad. Right, cotton varnishing cloth.

tive outer coat in a final process that may be either varnishing, wax filling or wax polishing.

Varnishing, wax filling, wax polishing

These processes are all carried out at room temperature (15−20°C).[2]

Varnishing and wax filling, which are parallel processes, call for the same preliminary application of filler. The two operations are performed with the aid of high-quality spirit between 95° and 99° proof (usually 95°, 99° being used for the final

71

48
Jacques Dubois and Pierre II Migeon, veneered desk, violet wood on an oak carcase, Paris, *c.* 1745 (0.83 by 1.98 by 1 m), restored in 1971. The colour of the pieces was killed with acid, the shine taken off the varnish with tripoli (Paris, Louvre Museum).

polish on varnish) at workshop temperature. It is used – alone or mixed with the varnish or wax – in a pad of white wool[3] wrapped in a piece of linen (no other material may be used) that is changed at each stage of the operation. Care must be taken not to soak the pad too thoroughly. Gentle pressure is applied to the freshly filled pad, gradually increasing as the pad empties. The heat of the restorer's hand causes the spirit to evaporate.[4] When the pad is dry and no longer slides it is refilled. In certain places (e.g. panels surrounded with mouldings, fluting), to prevent material from accumulating in the corners[5] the restorer uses a special polishing cloth that can be bought ready-made, looks like a piece of loose knitting, and is soaked and used in the same way as a wrapped pad.

Where small elements of dismantled furniture need to be filled and then varnished or waxed, it is best to fix them to a flat surface by nailing blocks round them or to glue them lightly to a piece of wood, which gives an even better hold.

49
Jean-François Oeben, roll-top secretaire, Paris, *c.* 1760 (0.98 by 0.82 by 0.52 m), restored in 1976. The top and the two sides, which had split, were closed up again. The contrast between the colours of the different woods (flowered scrolls on a sycamore ground, king-wood strings, rosewood borders, elements of green-dyed wood), which had faded on the surface, has been discreetly restored. The holes for fixing the band mounts (now removed) have been left visible. The piece has been varnished (Paris, Nissim de Camondo Museum).

FRENCH POLISHING

The method of varnishing known in the English-speaking world (though not in France) as 'French polishing' (ills. 47–9) enjoys an international reputation. It is performed in three stages: filling, varnishing and polishing. All these operations, which call for a great deal of experience and a wide knowledge of the types of wood being treated, are sometimes entrusted to a professional polisher. My feeling, however, is that it is better if the restorer does them himself. A prime necessity is that the atmosphere should be free of dust.

Filling

This involves plugging the pores of the wood to give it a smooth look and prepare the way for varnishing. Good filling is a *sine qua non* of a good finish. If the pores are not filled, the varnish will not grip; if they are inadequately filled they will absorb varnish and give a messy finish. Where the piece of furniture has been stained, the restorer rubs it down lightly before filling. He must be careful to avoid talc, plaster or any of the proprietary fillers (although the latter speed up the job considerably); they will cloud the varnish subsequently.

The best way to fill is with pumice, a volcanic rock, although it is a long and difficult process. The restorer can either grind his own pumice or buy it ready-ground. It comes in two grades: a very fine powder that is used throughout the operation and a coarser pumice in the form of very small grains that, contrary to appearances, do not scratch the wood and are used only at the early stages of the filling operation in conjunction with the finer grade. Surfaces to be filled must be placed horizontally to prevent the pumice from running.

Pumice is never put on the pad but is applied straight to the wood. It is spread by rubbing it in circles with a pad soaked in spirit. The spirit combines with the pumice to form a paste that gets into the pores, after which it evaporates.[6] After a while the restorer stops applying pumice and continues with spirit alone in order to dilute the paste and improve its penetration. Filling should not create a thickness; if it does, i.e. if any paste is left on the surface, the varnish will cloud. The operation ends when, looking at the surface against the light, the restorer can no longer make out any hollows where the pores occur.

If in the course of this operation further blemishes are found, they can still be corrected after the first application of filler. Any remaining small holes or cracks are stopped with coloured wax. There are tinted putties available but they may reject the varnish; it is best if the restorer melts down and tints his own beeswax fill. He applies it with a bone or wooden spatula, using this to remove any surplus afterwards. Having stopped the holes, he rubs down the wax with very fine glass-paper, which though it appears to turn it white in fact leaves the colour unaffected; it will be restored during the second stage of the filling process. The restorer then applies fine-grade pumice powder by hand, which will show him whether there is still any wax to be rubbed down. If there is, he will go over it again with glass-paper.

As it dries, the paste shrinks and consequently sinks slightly in the pores. After a minimum of one night, the filling process is completed by repeating the operation as before. If necessary a third application of filler can be made twenty-four hours later.

A piece of wood can be regarded as completely

filled when it is looked at against the light and the pores show up as small, dull, bluish spots. The surface is now perfectly smooth, without the slightest indentation, and is ready for varnishing.

Two applications of filler are usually sufficient on close-grained woods. Rosewood and violet wood fill well. Mahogany is porous and difficult to fill, some sorts more so than others; filling mahogany is an apparently endless task.

If varnish is applied immediately after filling, the pores will open up again. The paste must be left to dry for a day or two first. After that time, and after 'buffing' with very fine glass-paper or applying another light fill, the restorer can proceed to varnish immediately.

Where marquetry work is incised, the lines usually appear in black. They can be filled with charcoal dust. After rubbing down, the restorer first applies a light pumice and spirit fill, because if the charcoal is put on immediately it will darken the wood. He then inserts the charcoal and fills in the normal way. Incised work can also be filled with a putty made of dark wax.

Varnishing

The object of this is twofold: to heighten the gloss resulting from the filling operation by protecting it from the destructive effects of the atmosphere, and to embellish the wood by bringing out its figure and colour. Varnish necessarily forms a certain thickness, otherwise it will come off, but it must be kept as thin and transparent as possible. It preserves the colour of wood unaffected or darkens it only very slightly – unlike the thicker, oily type of varnish (known to the French as 'English varnish'), which forms a thin veil and deepens the colour.

Varnish is obtained by dissolving a resin in a volatile vehicle; the latter evaporates while the former hardens on contact with air and produces the desired effect. The varnish used by furniture restorers is based on shellac. Care must be taken not to use types of varnish that are inappropriate to antique furniture. Some restorers 'French polish' with cellulose varnishes, which go on much more quickly than shellac varnish but give a flashy finish. Polyester varnish, which forms as it were a sheet of glass over the surface and can only be removed with strippers that attack wood, is disastrous, particularly on veneered furniture.

Shellac varnish is available commercially but restorers usually make up their own recipe based on dissolving natural shellac in spirit and adding various ingredients. Such varnish is not tinted but always has a bit of colour due to the resin it contains in various shades. The most widely used type is white varnish, which occasionally goes yellow on the piece of furniture after a long time because the quality of shellac available is no longer what it was. Cherry shellac varnish is darker and does not alter. The operation can be speeded up by applying the varnish thickly, but thick varnish may obscure the colour of the wood and start to flake. Varnish needs to be applied very thinly and worked for a long time to make it stick to the surface and retain its gloss when dry.

A small surface is always more difficult to varnish: having applied the varnish one is in danger of removing it with the pad immediately afterwards. It is better to varnish a number of small elements at a time, going from one to another in order to give the varnish time to dry between rubs. Where elements of a dismantled piece are varnished separately, they will be given another rub after the piece has been reassembled. Glued mouldings are also best varnished separately and then reglued in position and given a final light rub. Another thing to look out for is not to use for varnishing a piece of linen that has previously been used for filling; it will contain a residue of pumice, which will cloud and scratch the varnish.

Varnishing in two stages, the restorer proceeds as follows (with certain variations). The pad is soaked in both varnish and spirit, the latter to deposit the former on the wood and allow it to dry there. The pad is then wrapped in linen and the contents kneaded well. It is important that the pad should not be too wet in case the varnish sticks, particularly at the beginning of the operation when it would tend to pick up the filler. To avoid leaving trails of varnish the restorer works the pad in circles and then in figures of eight, moving it less quickly than when filling in order to allow the varnish time to be deposited. The first rubbing will produce as high a gloss as can be obtained, but several coats are applied to make the finish more solid. When the surface is already covered with a thin film of varnish and the pad is beginning to catch, a few drops of vaseline oil on the linen will get it sliding better again without leaving marks. When the restorer thinks his varnish layer is thick enough, he gradually reduces the amount of varnish and finishes with spirit alone, polishing the varnish in order to dry out the oil and remove the pad marks. He must then leave it to dry for a minimum of twenty-four hours. As it dries it will shrink, and the operation will need to be repeated.

He will use this time for touching up, because one of the advantages of French polishing as far as re-storers are concerned is the scope it offers for touching up in the actual thickness of the varnish between the first and second coats. Some of them, seeing this as one of the more creative aspects of their profession, go a bit too far here. It is, however, quite admissible to disguise the outline of rather too obvious replacement pieces, the joints of slivers inserted into veneer, shellackings and perforations. This is done by daylight with the piece of furniture standing in its normal position, so enabling the restorer to judge the effect. It is the varnish one is touching up rather than the wood. The varnish used for this is tinted with pigments dissolved in spirit (see p. 71) and applied with as pointed a brush as possible.

Before re-applying varnish, the restorer rubs down with very fine, even worn glass-paper to remove any blemishes in the first coat and to even up his re-touching work. He then applies another coat of varnish as before, finishing with pure spirit. This second coat of varnish is followed by the actual polishing.

Polishing

This delicate – and lengthy – operation, designed to remove any imperfections from the varnish, pad marks, or oil that may be left or that may have risen to the surface, and at the same time to dry the varnish, is performed with the aid of a polishing pad used only for this purpose and wrapped in a piece of clean, fine linen. The pad contains a very little 99° spirit, and the restorer may add a few drops of benzoin, which will dissolve in the spirit and help to give the varnish a glossy, transparent look. The pad is worked very quickly in order to avoid scorching the varnish.

50
Charles Cressent (attrib.), commode with satin-wood trellis work and king-wood borders on a deal carcase, Paris, *c.* 1725 (0.85 by 1.32 by 0.69 m), restored in 1976. The veneer was finished with wax filling. The marble, which had disappeared, was replaced. The piece is marked *Delorme,* referring either to master cabinet-maker François Faizelot Delorme (d. 1768) or to his son Adrien, who became a master in 1748; it cannot have been made by them, but they probably restored it, possibly around 1745–9 as some of the mounts bear the stamp of a crowned C that was put on mounts between those two dates (Meaux, Bossuet Museum).

Antique furniture looks better with a slightly dull shine. When varnish is thoroughly dry the shine can be taken off it with powdered charcoal or tripoli, a siliceous earth that used to be sold in cakes and now comes in powdered form. These are spread on with a hare's foot or bristle brush. The job takes a very long time, and the restorer must be careful not to scratch the varnish or leave any material in the corners of mouldings. Alternatively, of course, varnish will tone down by itself after a certain length of time.

A point to remember is that when one has varnished the cross-pieces between drawers, any deposit that may form either above or below must be removed, otherwise it may hamper the drawer action and eventually tear off the veneer.

Reviving varnish

In a case where no regluing or replacement and consequently no stripping and rubbing down are necessary, it is possible to revive an old, worn varnish coat. This is done by rubbing it down very lightly, for example with powdered charcoal, or buffing it with very fine glass-paper, and adding another coat on top, provided one is certain that the new varnish is of the same composition as the old.

Alternatively it can be done with something called 'reviver', a liquid product that the restorer mixes up himself or that can be obtained ready for use from a cabinet-maker's supplier. Quite safe to use, reviver contains varying proportions of spirit, turpentine, oil, sulphuric acid, vinegar, tripoli and benzoin. These ingredients form a cloudy mixture that needs to be shaken before use. Placing a few drops on a piece of cotton waste or polishing cloth, the restorer rubs a small area at a time, which he afterwards dries with a piece of linen.

Some self-styled 'restorers' like to give old varnish a flashy look by wiping it with linseed-oil – a disastrous practice because if the varnish is at all worn or scratched the oil will get into the wood and stain it.

WAX FILLING

This method, which gives a duller finish than varnish polishing, also takes less time but is made slightly tricky by the sometimes dubious quality of the waxes available nowadays (ill. 50). Wax can be applied as soon as pumice filling is completed. The process is the same as for varnishing except that the pad is soaked in liquid wax – actually beeswax melted in turpentine. Otherwise it is worked in the same way as varnish, with spirit gradually taking the place of wax. The wax is allowed to dry afterwards and then polished with spirit.

The thing about varnish is that it preserves and protects wood better, shellac being a powerful insulator against dryness, damp, water, insects and mildew; and by making it possible to touch up the colour it means that one can conserve a maximum of original material. Wax will keep out insects, but since it does not form an actual layer touching up is more difficult; it needs a perfect surface without any shellacking, otherwise blemishes will show up. A piece of furniture that has been waxed will mark easily on contact with fingers, greasy substances and water. Wax filling is, however, easier to maintain than varnish because it can be revived simply by rubbing and treated with wax polish. It needs treating, too, because wood tends to suck wax in, and sometimes this can be a disadvantage, for example when the piece in question is decorated with mounts that have to be removed for the purpose.

In certain cases the restorer may hesitate over his choice of finish for a particular piece of antique furniture: would French polishing or wax filling be best? Both methods have their supporters, who regard one or the other finish as being the strongest and as setting wood off to the best advantage. Generally one varnishes veneered furniture and solid-wood furniture made of exotic timbers

(mahogany, for example). Wax filling is applied as a finish particularly to walnut and fruit woods but is also suitable for exotic veneers, provided they are not too badly damaged (unless of course it is intended to leave any repairs visible).

Whichever finish is adopted — and this will often depend on the state the wood is in — it may not necessarily be what the piece of furniture had to begin with, though one will try to get close to that, for example by using a mat varnish on furniture that was originally waxed. The latter solution lends

51
Tarsia certosina panels, walnut, inlaid with marquetry in oak, pear, plum, sycamore and box up to 3.5 mm in depth. Left to right:
— Panel I, unstripped, soiled by the wax having caught the dust.
— Panel II, stripped with an oil stripper. The place where the marquetry is to be reconstructed has been levelled off with a chisel. The worm damage will be stopped with tinted wax.
— Panel III (lower part). The incised work is being restored on the replacement pieces of pear wood; these will be coloured with water stains.
— Panels III (upper part) and IV. The wood has been waxed with a cork block and tinted wax, and its restoration is complete.

itself to solid-wood and veneered furniture made of an indigenous wood such as walnut, as long as there are not too many blemishes. Eighteenth-century French cabinet work was originally waxed and not usually varnished until the nineteenth century. At the end of the reign of Louis XV (1774) varnish would still appear to have been used only rarely. 'Cabinet work is hardly ever varnished; mostly it is just rubbed with wax,' wrote Watin in 1773,[7] and in the year of the king's death Roubo said of veneered furniture that 'the most usual sort of polish is that done with wax' (see pp. 58 f.). But he also pointed out that 'where cabinet work is not ordinarily polished with wax and the piece is important enough to justify the expense of a more handsome finish', this was achieved with tripoli and subsequently whiting, after which, 'since the majority of wood colours, whether from the Indies or from France, or stained woods lose their brightness with age and since it is very important to preserve those colours, one cannot do better [...] than to varnish them with white varnish', consisting of spirit and resins. 'Several coats of this varnish can be applied to cabinet work without risk of their obscuring the colours [...] This method of finishing cabinet work is a little more expensive and susceptible than the others, but it also has the advantage of being the most perfect, because varnish, by filling all the pores in the wood, captures its colour, and since varnish cannot evaporate that colour remains always in the same condition.'[8] The copies and pastiches of eighteenth-century furniture made in

Paris by Beurdeley, Dasson and Sormani in the late nineteenth century – work of irreproachable quality – were not varnished either but finished by wax filling.

WAX POLISHING

Solid-wood furniture made of oak, beech and possibly walnut does not need filling with the aid of spirit. The pores can be filled and a shine created by simply waxing directly. A gentle rub down is necessary first because the surface must be scrupulously clean; any dirt will reject the wax one is trying to put on top of it.

Wax polish is prepared by grating beeswax into a glass vessel, covering it with turpentine, and leaving it to steep until the wax has melted to form a homogeneous mixture. The resultant paste may be further diluted with petrol to make it liquid. It can also be lightly tinted. Depending on its consistency, it is applied with a brush, rag or cotton cloth. It must go right into the wood and not stay on the surface, otherwise it will leave the piece of furniture sticky and attract dust. After drying, the shine is brought up with a bristle, nylon or quill brush or, for the corners, a box burnisher, finishing off with a woollen cloth or chamois leather.

Waxing can also be done with a piece of cork. A cake of wax is rubbed over the surface in such a way as to leave a thin layer of wax on the wood, and this is then rubbed with a block of cork to work it into the pores and impart a polish (ill. 51).

BOULLE MARQUETRY

The term 'marquetry' alone was often used in seventeenth- and eighteenth-century France[1] to denote a technique that from the eighteenth century onward was associated particularly with the name of Boulle. It consists in veneering a soft-wood (usually deal) groundwork with motifs cut in the manner described above (see p. 49) from materials other than wood – copper or brass and tortoise-shell being the two most commonly used, but also including pewter, horn, ivory and mother-of-pearl. Natural red copper was used very much less than a brass alloy of approximately two-thirds copper to one-third zinc. The tortoise-shell was glued to paper and often coloured on the back, for example in red, either by applying a coat of paint to it or by using coloured paper.[2] Horn was also coloured on the verso, usually blue or green, and glued to paper. All these materials might in addition be incised with a burin, though this type of decoration will often have disappeared by now, particularly on tortoise-shell.

Perfected around 1660 in Germany and France, where André-Charles Boulle (1642–1732) was to take it to new heights a few years later, this kind of marquetry was used on luxury furniture until the early part of the eighteenth century. In France under Louis XV (1715–74) it was no longer used except on clock cases,[3] although furniture believed to be by Boulle continued to be greatly sought after. It came back into fashion more particularly under Louis XVI, when much furniture of the Louis XIV period was restored or copied. Finally, from about 1840 to the end of the nineteenth century the technique came back into use, particularly in Paris where during this period Mme Ledoux-Lebard counted more than 70 manufacturers of Boulle-style furniture,[4] and it represents an important current in the history of furniture.

Boulle marquetry is both the most fragile type of furniture decoration there is and the trickiest to restore. Damage, apart from that due to faults in the groundwork, stems particularly from the brass, which being impervious to glue adheres poorly to wood. When the wood shrinks, the brass comes unstuck, sometimes hanging on by no more than the bronze mouldings often placed round marquetry panels. Pewter tends to stick better than brass. Tortoise-shell is more able to match the movements of wood arising out of temperature fluctuations. It swells in damp conditions, however, lifts at the joint wherever two pieces are glued side by side, and

52
Seventeenth-century Boulle marquetry desk undergoing restoration. The top has been removed, revealing the deal carcase. Visible on the right is a panel (the left-hand side of the desk), the badly damaged marquetry of which has already been partly unglued. It is composed of brass and red-tinted tortoise-shell. Missing pieces of tortoise-shell had been touched out in places with red varnish by a previous restorer.

comes away with the brass, while the paper glued to the back of it comes unstuck or tears in its thickness. So whatever its date, Boulle marquetry work will have been many times restored. That of Louis XIV's time was restored very early on. In Paris in 1755 Duvaux invoiced some 'repairs made to a large Boulle desk, coffers and filing cabinets, renovating everything, 120 l.' In 1756 he repaired 'two marquetry wardrobes with missing pieces of brass and tortoise-shell supplied by the client, replaced

slivers on the sides and re-ebonized'.[5] Shortly afterwards, as we have seen, cabinet-makers were specializing in the restoration of such pieces – men like Nicolas-Pierre Séverin (1728–98) who worded his label: 'Séverin, dealer in cabinet work, Paris, known for the perfect restoration of furniture by the celebrated Boulle, has the honour to inform French and foreign collectors that he maintains a store of the aforesaid pieces...'[6] Riesener himself restored furniture of this type for the Crown Furniture Repository; in 1784 he charged 38 l. for 'mending and restoring a large Boulle wardrobe', and in 1785 he

53
Ungluing brass. In his right hand the restorer has a syringe full of spirit, which he allows to run over and under the metal, lifting this with a blade held in his left hand.

54
Ungluing tortoise-shell. The glue is gradually softened with a damp rag that is gently heated with an iron. The red paint on the verso of the tortoise-shell cannot be salvaged.

charged 240 l. for 'repairing and renovating a large desk in old Boulle marquetry, restoring the carcase and the marquetry as well as the gilding'.[7] We find Boulle pieces stamped after restoration by Riesener, Séverin and other cabinet-makers of the period: Dubois, Montigny, Weisweiler, Delorme and Levasseur. In 1823, however, the younger Levasseur was said to be possibly the only man in Paris capable of repairing Boulle furniture. But from the reign of Louis-Philippe onward the *Almanach du Commerce* was reporting of various manufacturers of Boulle furniture that they also undertook restoration work; around 1850, for example, one Caillaux receives the mention: 'Cabinet-maker, inlayer,

manufacturer of Boulle-style furniture, repair of mounts [...] repair of Boulle furniture, wooden marquetry.'[8]

Such repairs were occasionally carried out by not particularly scrupulous craftsmen, who for example were quite prepared to disguise the disappearance of pieces of tortoise-shell with the aid of red varnish, that of pieces of brass with gilded wax, and that of pewter by melting new metal into the holes. Many cabinet-makers even nowadays hesitate to restore Boulle marquetry work; it is invariably a very lengthy process, and they feel it will only need redoing in a few years' time.

I said in connection with restoring veneer that one must unglue as little as possible. Boulle marquetry, however, by virtue of the materials it employs, is a rather special case; often the restorer finds it in such bad shape that partial regluing is out of the question and a more radical approach is unavoidable. Taking the most common case – that of a piece of furniture veneered in brass and tortoise-shell – I would venture to suggest the following measures. There are in fact two possible solutions: either one removes all the marquetry or one removes only the metal.

Removing all the marquetry

UNGLUING

Before the restorer starts ungluing the marquetry he must take a carbon impression of the panel to be treated (ill. 52). The panel is then brushed with water. He first removes the brass, which comes away more easily (with 95° spirit), working the blade (ill. 53) slowly in case he encounters any of the often invisible pins that some cabinet-makers

55
Close-up of the panel being unglued in ill. 52. On the left the marquetry is still in place (the brass wing of the bird has lifted); this is *première partie* Boulle work, with brass motifs in a tortoise-shell ground; the brass is incised. On the right the marquetry has been unglued; only traces of glue and paper remain on the groundwork.

were in the habit of driving into the brass or into the joints in order to fix the metal more firmly to the groundwork. He then unglues the tortoise-shell, either with a damping cloth and a hot iron, controlling both heat and humidity carefully to stop the tortoise-shell from buckling (ill. 54), or alternatively with spirit if this works. If the tortoise-shell has been coloured with paint and this has paper glued underneath it, the restorer will try to make the separation in the thickness of the paper in order to keep the original colouring. Often, however, this paint layer is too thin to be salvageable. As the pieces of brass and tortoise-shell are lifted they are held in position with pieces of gummed paper.

It is sometimes possible to use spirit to unglue brass

56
Reconstructing a marquetry panel. The unglued pieces missing in the last illustration have been mounted one by one on a tracing of the panel taken before the operation began. Note the lacunae.

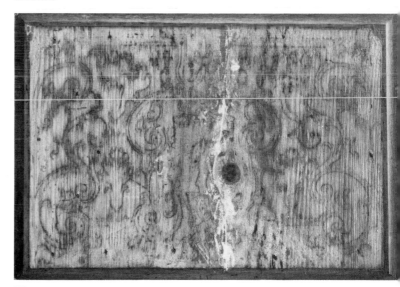

57
Repairing the groundwork. The split visible in ill. 55 has been filled with wood pulp.

and tortoise-shell simultaneously, for example on small panels, which makes reconstruction that much easier. Where a fragment comes away with the brass and tortoise-shell still interlocked, the restorer immediately covers the outer face with gummed paper. Sometimes the glue remains in the joints, which avoids the necessity for filling the kerf or gap left by the saw-blade at the cutting stage.

Any brass motifs that have become distorted will need to be beaten flat with a small hammer either directly or between two metal cauls. Tortoise-shell buckled by the ungluing process need only be heated slightly with steam and left to cool under a caul. Fragments of paper and glue will be left on the backs of the pieces of brass and tortoise-shell; these the restorer must scrape off, taking care not to damage the paint on the back of the tortoise-shell where this is still good. Where it has gone he moistens the back of the tortoise-shell with a brush or sponge dipped in hot water, scrapes off all the glue and paper, and cleans the surface thoroughly in preparation for a fresh coat of paint. As each piece or section is removed it is arranged in position on the carbon impression of the panel, with the restorer using his fingers, a blade or a point to fit them into one another. In this way he gradually builds up the whole panel, holding it together with criss-crossing strips of gummed paper (ills. 55–8). When the process is complete, gummed paper is applied to the back of the marquetry and that on the front removed to allow the restorer to work on it.

REPLACING MISSING PIECES
Another carbon impression is made of the unglued panel for any missing pieces of tortoise-shell or brass that may need replacing.

By and large the restoration of Boulle marquetry does not involve the same problems of matching as restoring wooden marquetry occasionally presents, though it may be difficult to find exactly the right tortoise-shell.

Replacement pieces of tortoise-shell can be prepared as follows. The piece of unpolished tortoise-shell (ill. 59) is smoothed off with a scraper on the side that looks cleanest (often the scraper will reveal small holes in the material) and afterwards rubbed down with glass-paper. The dust from the rubbing down is carefully collected. A further rub down with wet emery-paper gives an almost polished surface that the restorer Scotch-glues to a piece of plywood. The same thing is then done to the other side, where the tortoise-shell is scraped down to the required thickness. The tortoise-shell used on seventeenth- and eighteenth-century furniture – from the hawk's-bill turtle – is thicker than 'turtle-shell' that was used in the nineteenth century.[9] The tortoise-shell is then unglued from the plywood with the aid of steam or hot water. Tortoise-shell can be bent into any shape when hot and will retain that shape on cooling. Pieces of tortoise-shell can also be welded together: the edges to be joined are bevelled in opposite directions and fitted together; the pieces are then welded by sandwiching them between sheets of paper and pressing them between hot copper cauls by means of a clamp.

Before cutting out the pieces, the restorer will of course select his new tortoise-shell to match the surviving material as closely as possible. If the original tortoise-shell is untinted or if it needs to be retinted completely, the original colour having disappeared when the pieces were unglued, the piece of new tortoise-shell is Scotch-glued to a thin sheet of plywood

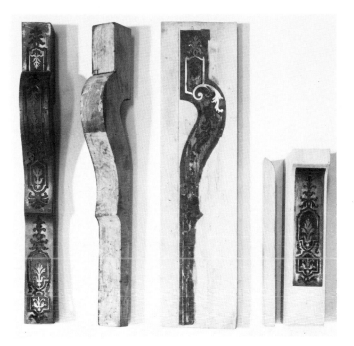

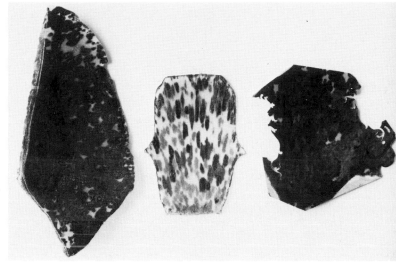

58
Restoration of the consoles at the corners of the same desk. Left to right: one of the consoles before restoration, with some of the brass pieces hanging on by only a few points; another console, from which the marquetry has been unglued; reconstituted marquetry panel from one side of this last console, seen from the back (note the new brass motifs in the upper part); reconstructed panel from the outer face of the same console, with shaped caul and counter-caul.

59
Unpolished tortoise-shell. Left to right: from hawk's-bill turtle; 'turtle-shell'; piece of hawk's-bill shell glued to plywood with the marquetry pieces already cut out.

(1.5 or 3 mm thick) and this in turn is glued to a piece of thick cardboard or veneer in order to prevent the whole thing from buckling and to make it easier for the restorer to cut his replacement motifs. If on the other hand he has been able to salvage the red paint (or whatever colour it may be), the restorer tints a quantity of vinyl adhesive to the required shade, adding some of the powdered tortoise-shell kept from the rubbing-down process if the original paint is thick in texture. It is a good idea

to test one's tinted adhesive first because the colour may change as it dries. The restorer then uses this preparation to glue the sheet of tortoise-shell to a piece of Bristol board that is itself glued to a piece of plywood that the restorer has first counterbalanced on the verso in the manner described above.

Once all the adhesive is dry, the tortoise-shell is covered with very thin Scotch glue or paste and the cut-out patterns for the replacement pieces are stuck on and sawn round with a marquetry saw. This done, the patterns are moistened with hot water and scraped off. Where the tortoise-shell has been glued straight to the plywood it need only be plunged into hot water for a moment to unglue it. If not it is separated from the plywood by sliding a paring knife or old razor through the thickness of the Bristol board – very carefully in order to avoid nicking the tortoise-shell – and the remaining Bristol board is then scraped off to expose the paint. Restoring the colour of tortoise-shell (or of horn, for that matter) is a slightly vexed question. How can one be sure that the piece of furniture one is restoring still has its original colour? This may have changed with age or been altered during a previous restoration. Roubo writes that tortoise-shell was often coloured red in his day. But was this not done more systematically in the nineteenth century? When in doubt, the wise course is to reproduce the colour that has come down to us. Where, however, the restorer feels he is dealing with original colouring matter that is going to be lost when he unglues the pieces, he may have it analysed in order to find out whether or not it has faded, and then possibly restore it as it was.

Brass, like red copper and pewter, comes in the form of large sheets. The gauge selected will depend on that of the tortoise-shell but will average between $5/10$ and $6/10$, though a $7/10$ gauge is preferable wherever possible. The restorer cuts the sheet into smaller pieces, which he will need to reheat in order to make them easier to saw. As with tortoise-shell, the patterns for the replacement pieces are glued on the brass, which is itself glued to a piece of plywood, and sawn out. Small pieces of metal can be removed from the plywood backing simply by sliding a blade between the two; larger pieces can be left to soak in hot water. If necessary the pieces of brass are flattened as described above.

If the pieces are to go on curved portions of the groundwork, brass ones are hammered into shape and tortoise-shell ones are plunged into hot water and bent. Both brass and tortoise-shell replacement pieces may need adjusting with a file to make them fit exactly. They are inserted into place with the fingers or, if they are very small, with tweezers. Any tiny pieces of tortoise-shell that may still be missing can be touched out with red shellac, which makes a passable imitation; the more this is heated, the darker it goes, so that one can match a shade pretty exactly.

When the whole panel has been reconstructed (ill. 60), the restorer covers the outer face with broad strips of gummed paper and removes those that were holding it together on the verso.

Where it is a question of replacing an entire panel of marquetry by copying a similar panel, the restorer takes a piece of 3 mm plywood and first glues the sheet of tortoise-shell to it, then the sheet of brass, and on top of that the pattern (ill. 61).

Whether he has replaced the whole panel or merely completed it, the restorer will now need to prepare a tinted putty in order to fill, on the verso, the kerf or saw cut between the brass and the tortoise-shell (unless, as we saw above, he has contrived to unglue them together).[10] Doing this from the verso avoids having the glue come up through the veneer when it is pressed and also, when it is necessary to replace colour under the tortoise-shell, having lines of that colour outlining the motifs. The putty is applied to all the joints with a spatula and goes right down into the cracks, any surplus being wiped off with a rag dipped in hot water. Still working on the verso, the restorer can give the brass more purchase on the groundwork by scratching it either with glass-paper (if it is uniformly thick all over) or with suitable tools (ill. 62). If the tortoise-shell needs colouring, he can then paint the whole of the back of the panel, using for example a red gouache from a tube, very lightly diluted and applied with a brush.

LEVELLING OFF

The next step is to eliminate any differences in thickness between brass and tortoise-shell, between the different pieces of either material, or between original and replacement pieces. The method described below makes it possible to do this without reducing the thickness of the marquetry and without affecting any incised work, because the operation is performed on the verso. First a sheet of thick paper is glued to the verso with vinyl adhesive. If the tortoise-shell is coloured red, red paper can be used

60
Completed reconstruction of the right-hand side of the same desk. It is held together with gummed paper on the verso. The missing pieces have been replaced (note the lighter, new brass).

and the adhesive can also be tinted with a little red pigment. The panel is placed face downward on a zinc or aluminium caul or a hardwood board with the usual protective sheet of paper between them. The verso is now covered with a sheet of fairly soft cardboard and the whole sandwich placed under a press. Where the marquetry is thicker the cardboard

61
Total renewal of a panel of marquetry to go on a leg of the same desk. Left: tortoise-shell, brass, and the pattern to be cut out are glued one on top of another to a piece of plywood; they are still there on the upper part. Centre: tortoise-shell and brass motifs belonging to the lower part, already cut out and separated. Right: another leg on which the identical marquetry work, already renewed, has been glued in place.

will give, and where it is thinner it will still be pressed flat against the caul. When the panel is removed from the press the face will be quite flat, whereas any unevennesses will show up in relief in the paper glued to the verso (ill. 63) and can be removed with glass-paper. At the end of the operation the paper behind the tortoise-shell motifs will usually still be there and that behind the brass motifs will usually be gone; what is important is that the surface will be true.

REGLUING
All traces of paper and glue must be removed from the groundwork.

There are serious problems about the type of glue to use for refixing Boulle marquetry. Scotch glue is fine for tortoise-shell, of course, but modern living conditions show it to be inadequate when it comes to fixing brass. Some restorers, when they are merely regluing the metal without removing the tortoise-shell, use an epoxy adhesive – a solution I find too radical. Boulle marquetry that was reglued with vinyl adhesive in the Louvre's restoration workshop some ten years ago has so far proved satisfactory. The adhesive, tinted red or not as the case may be, is brushed on to the groundwork and the back of the veneer. The restorer selects his cauls and method of pressing to suit the shape and dimensions of the panel concerned and keeps it in the press for 24 hours.

FINISHING
With the panel glued in position, any fixing pins are removed and any remaining traces of gummed paper scraped off the surface of the marquetry. Some cabinet-makers, as we have seen, liked to fix the brass more firmly than glue alone could do by driving pins through it into the groundwork. Roubo refers to the practice,[11] and one does in fact come across it occasionally on antique furniture. It may have been all right then, when furniture was not subjected to such variations of temperature and

62
Detail of the verso of the panel shown in ill. 60. The panel is now held together with gummed paper glued to the face. The kerf between brass and tortoise-shell has been filled. The brass has been scratched, except in the corner.

63
Levelling the panel shown in ill. 52. The outer face is now flat but differences of level have become apparent in the paper glued to the verso; these will now be eliminated.

humidity; nowadays it is best avoided and the metal left free.

It is at this stage that any incised work can be restored, provided always that the restorer has sufficient information at his disposal to enable him to complete the worn portions without having to invent. Pewter is easier to incise than brass. The incisions can be filled with glue tinted with lampblack or a little gouache; this is applied with a spatula and levelled off when dry. Other possible fills are dark wax and a mixture of Indian ink and shellac.[12]

An interval of several days should be left between regluing and rubbing down to allow the glue time to dry properly. The restorer rubs down as little as possible (taking care not to perforate the tortoiseshell), using progressively finer grades of glasspaper or wet emery-paper, the grain of which is finer still. Polishing is done with tripoli and then with powdered charcoal, both applied with an oily rag, possibly finishing off with polishing paste, also applied with a rag.

Finally the whole panel is given a rubbing of shellac varnish to prevent the brass from oxidizing. Some restorers wipe the brass with sulphydrate of ammonia before varnishing to give it an 'aged' look, but there is a risk of this leaving bluish stains and the practice is to be condemned.

64
The panel shown in ill. 52 glued back into place.

GILDING AND PAINTWORK

Gilding

Gilding on wood, which involves applying gold-leaf to a specially prepared surface, has always been done by specialist craftsmen. In pre-revolutionary Paris, gilders did not belong to the wood-working trades but formed a section of the guild of master painters and sculptors known as the Académie de Saint-Luc. At the beginning of this century the trade still comprised three distinct and separate specialists, corresponding to the three stages of the process: the sizer, the trimmer – who was the aristocrat of the profession – and the gilder proper. Nowadays the gilder usually does the lot. Gilders still acknowledge as their master the Parisian gilder Watin, author of *L'Art du peintre, doreur, vernisseur* ('The Art of the Painter, Gilder and Varnisher'), first published in 1772 and since reissued many times.

There are two types of gilding: water gilding and oil gilding. The great beauty of the former lies in the trimming or carving done in the gesso ground and the contrasts between mat and burnished areas of gold-leaf. The latter, cheaper method can sometimes be trimmed but never burnished, so that it presents a more uniform appearance.

WATER GILDING

Water gilding, in use in Italy since the Middle Ages and applied to luxury furniture almost all over Europe from the seventeenth century onward, is very solid and should normally be in a good state of preservation. The ground, which is stippled rather than spread on, adheres powerfully to wood, while gold itself is in principle non-corroding. Nevertheless a piece of gilded furniture will inevitably have lost something of its original brightness. Possibly because of the small amount of copper it always contains, gold darkens slightly with age. On the other hand it also wears away in places, exposing the clay bed and diminishing the contrast between mat and burnished areas to such an extent that the latter are sometimes difficult to make out at all.

Many other factors contribute to the deterioration of gilding. In the first place the wood underneath is subject to worm damage,[1] play, and all the usual accidents such as joints opening up, as they so often do at the corners of seats and consoles, for example. Here again the environment in which the piece is kept can do a great deal of harm. If it is too dry and

93

the wood shrinks, the rigid ground, unable to move with it, will begin to lift and may eventually flake away, taking the gilding with it. Nineteenth-century grounds tend to be more susceptible to lifting than older ones. Damp is another enemy, and gilding may be damaged as a result of having been cleaned with products containing water, or for example corroded around the inside of a mirror frame because the mirror has been cleaned repeatedly with a damp cloth. For all these reasons gilding has often needed restoring at a very early stage: 'Chatard will come and make good the 6 easy chairs and 2 bergères that are to go in the King of Sweden's cabinet at Versailles,' reads an order issued in 1784 in connection with some nearly new gilded furniture, and in 1787 the same gilder, Chatard, did a 'complete restoration job' on the gilded wooden furniture in Marie-Antoinette's bedroom at Versailles – furniture manufactured a mere eighteen years previously.[2]

Ever since the second third of the nineteenth century, over-zealous restoration of gilding that was regarded as ruined has seriously prejudiced our knowledge of the history of this form of decoration. In some cases the wood was stripped down and left in the natural state. In other cases worn gilding was covered with coats of paint – e.g. the black paint applied to Louis XV chairs during the Second Empire – in order to pass the piece off as modern. And lastly, gilding was often completely redone. In 1847 Balzac, writing about the dealer Elie Magus, mentions that 'The pictures, some hundred of them, were mounted in the most splendid frames, all delightfully regilded by the only gilder in Paris whom Elie judged to be conscientious, namely Servais, whom the old Jew taught to gild with English gold, a metal infinitely superior to that produced by French gold-beaters.'[3]

Regilding was done by different methods, depending on whether the wood was stripped down and a fresh ground prepared or whether the new ground and gilding were put on top of what was left of the old. In either case the gilding was not always water gilding. Sometimes only the relief portions, which were burnished, were regilded using the water process, the mat portions being done with mordant.[4] Or it might be that the whole piece was regilded by the mordant or oil method. Another method was bronze gilding, using powdered bronze in varnish, glue or turpentine, which was brushed on and left to oxidize. And some originally two-tone, white and gold pieces were gilded all over.[5]

Modern water gilding may have been well done, but more often than not it will have greatly impaired the look of the piece, gilding methods having changed slightly in the nineteenth century. Carved work was covered with more ground, which tended to clog it. Originally mat backgrounds were covered, as the

65

Louis XIV torchère (1.82 by 0.62 m), restored in 1972. The original gilding had been covered with a white ground and oil gilding; later on this in turn had been covered with several coats of paint. Stripping removed the paintwork and the oil gilding, and the modern ground was scraped off to reveal the badly damaged original gilding. Keeping the original ground and trimming (note the barleycorn motif in the mat portions), the torchère was regilded and deliberately not patinated (Paris, Notre-Dame-de-Bonne-Nouvelle church).

66

Leg of a Louis XVI chair. It is covered with late gilding in poor condition; this is about to be removed, a spot check having shown that the original gilding is still there underneath.

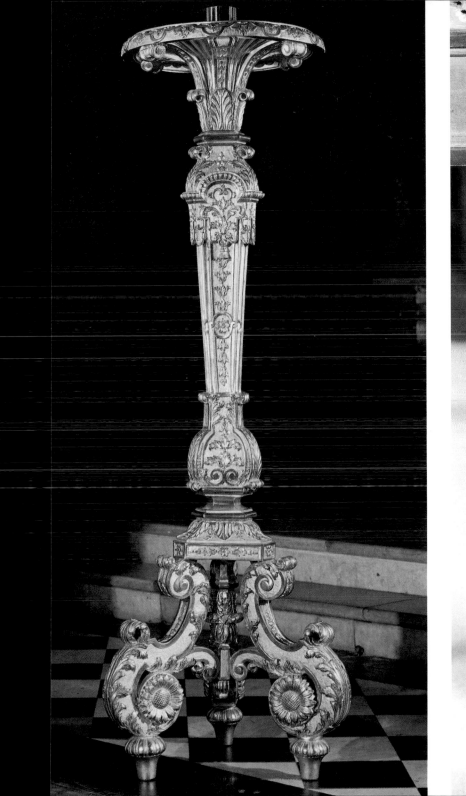

reliefs were, with several layers of bed; the whole thing was then burnished and the piece became shiny all over. Restorers may also have elaborated the carving by adding motifs in stucco. The trimming, even when done well – and sometimes it was done too well, in fact – failed to capture the spirit of the original. Nowadays these errors can and should be avoided.

A spot check will in some cases reveal that the old gilding is still there under the later layers. These will need to be stripped away, as already indicated (ills. 66–7). Where original gilding has survived in poor condition, the restorer has the grave responsibility of deciding whether to remove the lot or to save what is left, even if this is very little. Many restorers today agree with their nineteenth-century predecessors that complete regilding is the only answer where the old gilding has suffered damage. Clearly, too, it is easier than trying to restore. (Stripping damaged gilding to leave the bare wood is an even more serious step, for it means robbing an object that was designed to be gilded of the greater part of its attraction, namely the delicate trimming work and the subtle play of different textures of gold, which will be lost forever.) Rather than regild a piece completely, however, it is better to preserve old gilding no matter how worn as long as it still adheres, and if it does not to consolidate and complete it as far as possible. Here again, though, the restorer must avoid being dogmatic – and he must keep his wits about him as well: some modern work

67
Leg of the same chair after stripping. Removal of the later, uniform gilding has revealed the mat and burnished effects of the original gilding. Some patching will be necessary.

is far from solid, so that not every worn piece of gilding is necessarily old, nor need it be preserved at all costs.

If the piece has already been regilded in a satisfactory manner, it is better to preserve and restore this later gilding than to risk stripping down again; a second regilding would not recover any more of the original trimming.

The restoration of old gilding may involve a number of operations:

Restoring the woodwork

This must be done by a craftsman who is used to working with gilded wood in order not to aggravate the damage to the gilding. It should be stressed again that the piece of furniture should not be dismantled if this is anyhow avoidable.

Cleaning

Where gilding has been exposed by stripping, no further treatment is needed; the stripper itself will have cleaned it adequately.

In other cases, getting rid of the dirt covering the patina must be done with the very greatest care. It is impossible to say in advance what product will be most effective. Though often recommended, the practice of cleaning with a mixture of egg white and Javel water (bleach and disinfectant) is to be condemned; used without adequate experience, it may well remove the gold completely.

It is best to clean gilding with water containing a little rabbit-skin glue – the glue traditionally associated with the gilding process. Using an oil stripper (see p. 34) involves a greater degree of risk; it may remove the patina and give the gilding a flashy look. The restorer will use the same solution of water and glue to try and revive the burnish, because in fact old burnish cannot always be reburnished, the patina tending to make it go black.

Refixing flakes

The restorer will now go over the surface with his fingers to check whether the surviving gilding still holds. In some cases, particularly in the middle of very visible areas that are otherwise in good condition, any flaking material can be refixed, which will avoid the necessity for patching. Simply brushing glue over such flaking areas, however, is not enough. The restorer must lift them with a spatula or even remove them completely, injecting rabbit-skin glue with a syringe behind them and pressing them down with his finger.

Patching

If certain places have become impossible to reglue because the gilding has disintegrated, all loose material must be removed and in those places the restorer will proceed to carry out some or all of the numerous operations that together make up the gilding process. 'What is one to say', writes Watin, 'of those who are bold enough to claim that they can bring the gold back even in places from which it has disappeared? Yet somewhere I have read of methods for doing just this; but the best and surely the safest method is, when one is cleaning gilded work and observes that certain portions are absolutely bare of gold, to apply fresh gold, using to this end the process we have outlined for its application in the first instance.'[6] The restorer does nothing to the ground where this is in good condition, but he will need to add more clay size for the bed, recapturing the original colour, and he will of course

68
Detail of a carved table that was designed to be gilded.

replace the missing gold. It is essential to clean the areas around lacunae to prevent them from darkening at the burnishing stage; this is done by degreasing them with water and varnishing spirit or methylated spirits.

Complete renewal of gilding

Obviously there will be cases where the old gilding is in such a bad way that both refixing and patching are out of the question. The only solution is to regild completely, having first taken the precaution of keeping a sample of the original clay bed and gold-leaf in order to match them for colour. Ideally one is able to retain the original trimming (ill. 65).

On the other hand one is of course tempted to regild

natural wood that shows traces of ground in the hollows or 'depths', as they are called, or wood that, though now covered with mediocre paintwork or modern gilding, one believes must have been gilded originally. It is sometimes difficult to spot whether a piece of wood was originally gilded or painted. The appearance of the carving when stripped may serve as a guide. Wood to be gilded was carved more deeply than wood destined to receive the thinner covering of paint. The carving also has a dry, abrupt look because of the tendency of gilding to round out the surface. Finally certain details – e.g. the veins of leaves – are left out because they were trimmed into the ground at a later stage (ill. 68). This makes it difficult, however, to regild wood that has been stripped, because the gilder has to redo the trimming.

Perhaps this is the place to run through the different operations involved in gilding (ill. 69), particularly to clarify what has just been said.

First a few general principles. The surface being worked on must always be clean, and the same strength of glue must be used throughout each operation, a weaker solution being used for sizing and for laying down the bed of burnish clay. Gilders use rabbit-skin glue, made from animal cartilege and skin, and they use it hot (ill. 70).[7]

Degreasing

The first step is to degrease the wood with alkali or warm vinegar, which has the additional advantage

69
The various stages of water gilding. White ground or gesso (right); ochre size over the ground; brown bed laid on the relief portions; gold-leaf fixed to the bed (lower part).

70
Some of the gilder's materials and equipment. Right, a slab of rabbit-skin glue. Centre, three cakes of burnish clay or bed (black, red and yellow), three polishing stones, scouring rushes. Left, boxwood polishing stick.

of raising the pores, thus allowing the size to penetrate better.

Sizing
This prepares the wood for the layers of ground and also has the effect of consolidating worm-eaten wood. Hot, very liquid glue (some restorers add a little garlic) is applied with a brush. This glue or size is lightly tinted with whiting to enable one to see when the surface is completely covered. If the pores are still raised, a second coat of size may be applied.

Ground
The purpose of this is to insulate and at the same time even out the surface of the wood. Its importance cannot be exaggerated, because if it is poorly executed the gilding will flake off. It adheres less

well to walnut, which is a very close-grained wood. This ground or 'gesso', as it is sometimes called, is a mixture of glue size and whiting that can be made up in advance but that must be identical throughout the operation; if the different coats are not all of the same strength, the ground will crack. The mixture is heated in a double boiler and while in use is kept at a constant temperature, otherwise it will stiffen. For the same reason it must be applied in a warm atmosphere (minimum temperature 20°C).

The ground is applied with a brush (ill. 71), using a stippling action to avoid clogging the depths and leaving more material on areas to be trimmed than on smooth areas. Less ground is needed on gilding from the Louis XIV and Régence periods than on Louis XV gilded work, in which trimming plays a more important part. The mixture sets very quickly and must be applied to only a small area at a time. The first coat is fairly thin and worked well into the depths; the following coats (five or six, until the wood is really well covered) are thicker except for the final, lighter one. It is very important to wait until one coat has dried before applying the next, though unfortunately this is not always done. The best method of drying is by sunlight, provided that it is not too strong.

As he applies his ground the restorer fills any worm-holes or splits in the wood with a putty made from the same materials as the ground – glue and whiting – but with less glue to make it less liquid.[8] This is put on with a roughing chisel and must be left for about 12 hours to dry thoroughly. A dry surface does not necessarily mean that the putty is dry right through, and if it is not the moisture may work its way through the ground and eventually cause flaking.

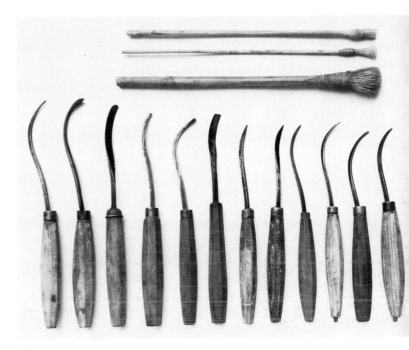

71
Above, large brushes for stippling the ground. Below, trimming irons in a variety of shapes.

The last coat of gesso is smoothed off with a brush dipped in warm water, or – more traditionally – moistened with saliva, since there is a danger of water diluting the glue. The restorer then proceeds to rub down. Here the traditional scouring rush[9] is nowadays often replaced by very fine glass-paper, which is equally effective, though the former may still be used for the more inaccessible places. Another tool used is the polishing stick, either on its own or in conjunction with a scouring rush. For mat areas on Louis XVI furniture (fluting, flat surfaces) the restorer uses polishing stones, which are artificial stones sold in cake form and sawn up (ill. 70).

Trimming

The ground is now trimmed with curved metal tools (ills. 71–2) in order to bring out the carving obscured by the gesso ground and perhaps to complete it by adding a few lines and by ornamenting the depths of carved motifs such as barleycorn (ill. 65), this latter operation giving the gilder scope for a certain amount of independent creation.[10] The surface is then cleaned again with a sponge and clean water or rubbed lightly with glass-paper to soften the effect of the trimming.

Ochre sizing

The purpose of this is to mask places where it may not be possible to get gold right into the depths; it also serves as a mordant for the clay bed and to hold the gold-leaf. It consists of a thin size mixture (one part glue to six parts water) coloured with yellow ochre and sometimes with a brushful of the burnish clay used for the bed. Any grains or lumps must be carefully filtered out, and the mixture must not be too warm in case it softens the ground. Ochre size is applied with a brush – generously, to get it well into the depths. The surplus is then dabbed off with a sponge and the size allowed to dry.

The bed

A bed of so-called 'burnish clay' is then applied to take the gold-leaf and enable the restorer (or of course the gilder) to burnish it afterwards. Burnish clay used to come in the form of cakes of various

72
Trimming. This is done in the ground with the aid of carving tools, but these are used in the opposite direction.

73
The gilder's tool kit. Left to right: gilder's cushion or 'cush' of still-born calf's skin (to which gold does not adhere), draught-proofed with a piece of flexible parchment; 'book' of gold-leaf; knife for cutting leaf; gilder's tip for picking it up; gilder's bucket with two damping brushes; three brushes for pressing down (the largest one being also used for dusting off afterwards); double-ended brush, one end for picking up tiny pieces of gold-leaf, the other for pressing them down.

colours – black, blue, green, yellow, red (ill. 70) – that could be mixed before use. Italian gilders often used a yellow bed, English gilders a black one. In France it was reddish to give the gold a warmer tone, darker in the eighteenth century, lighter in the nineteenth. It contained various substances but mainly an ochreous clay known as 'Armenian bole', which French gilders obtained from quarries in Burgundy, the Loire valley and the Paris region, particularly at Meudon. Some years ago the French firm that used to supply this traditional bed lost its sources and Armenian bole became unobtainable. After experimenting for several years it eventually came up with a substitute bed based on pipe clay[11] tinted red with iron oxide. The new product is not as good as the traditional one, however, and it surely ought to be possible to resume working the old Armenian bole quarries.

Some restorers still have supplies of the old bed. It is prepared as follows:

The cake of clay is soaked in water and then, turning it, the gilder or restorer adds thin glue (if the glue is too strong the burnish will be poor). Gradually the glue takes the place of the water, which rises to the surface of the mixture. This surplus water must be removed each day and replaced with an equal quantity of glue. Once prepared, the bed is kept in an earthenware pot. It must not be used for a week after preparation, but it can then be used for some time.

The modern pipe-clay bed was first sold in cakes, but people complained that it was gritty. It now comes in the form of a paste and no longer needs to be soaked; thinned out with glue, it can be used straight away.

It is vital that the restorer matches the colour of the original bed, particularly when he is patching. Where he can no longer obtain the old type of bed in the various colours, he will have to tint a red clay bed with gouache – adding ultramarine blue, for example, to match certain old French beds, and, to brighten the colour, a dash of carmine.

The bed must be very liquid and smooth to avoid creating a thickness, and the long brush with which it is laid on must be cleaned very carefully. Some gilders lay one thick bed to save time, but it is better to lay several thin ones. Burnish clay may be applied to areas that it is intended to leave mat, but this is not essential. Areas to be burnished will need two or three beds, each one being allowed to dry before the next is laid on top. At the end of the operation the bed can be fixed by wiping it with a little Formol.

Gilding

In France there are two firms that, thanks to parallel industrial activities, still hand-beat gold to some extent. Other countries – Germany, Italy, England, Japan – supply gold-leaf produced by more or less mechanized methods.[12] It is a good idea for the restorer to have a selection of gold-leaf from different sources to enable him to match for colour when he is patching. Gold-leaf – lemon yellow, green, red and various shades in between – is usually 22 carat. It comes in 80, 84 or 93 mm squares, the second size (which is the one gold-leaf always used to come in) being particularly suitable for patching. Modern gold-leaf is thinner – 0.1 to 0.8 microns – than it was in the eighteenth and nineteenth centuries: 'Our forbears used much thicker gold,' wrote Watin back in 1772.[13] The leaves are arranged in 'books' of 25. If you are employing a restorer, make sure he does not use machine-beaten copper or aluminium leaf instead of gold, because these will age after only a few months.

The actual laying of the gold-leaf (ill. 73) is a fairly rapid operation compared with what has gone before. The gilder arranges a sheet of gold-leaf on his 'cush', as the special leather gilder's cushion is called, and blows it flat; if he only wants to use part of it he cuts out what he wants with a knife. Near him he has his bucket (also a rather special piece of equipment) containing water at room temperature

74
Agate burnishing stones.

75
Burnishing. Note the thumb of the left hand carefully controlling the stone to stop it burnishing portions that are to remain mat.

together with a little glue and possibly also a little spirit to speed up drying and get rid of any grease. This mixture, known as 'laying water', will need to be changed from time to time as it gets too much burnish clay in it. Laying water is brushed on to the area to be gilded,[14] moistening the bed that is to hold the gold-leaf. Drawing the tip either through his hair or over his cheek, where he will have first dabbed a little grease (lady gilders do this on their forearm), the gilder uses it to pick the leaf up and place it in position. He works from left to right (if he is right-handed), doing the parts to be left mat first and the parts to be burnished afterwards; this is to keep any laying water off the latter, because it would stain them and prevent the burnish from coming up. The leaves are made to overlap slightly. Often, particularly in uneven places or when the leaf does not spread properly, it is pressed down with a special brush. For gilding small areas, the tiny pieces of gold-leaf needed are picked up with a particularly fine brush.

How long gilding takes to dry depends on the ground and on the temperature of the surroundings; also some areas may dry more quickly than others. In general it needs to be left for two or three hours before burnishing. Once the gilding is dry, it is dusted off with a large brush. Some restorers occasionally gild twice to give a better burnish; for patching work this has the advantage of reproducing the thickness of the original gilding.

Burnishing

A small quantity of grease is applied to the area to be burnished in order to make the agate burnishing stone (ills. 74–5) slide better. Italian gilders sometimes burnished the depths. In eighteenth-century France only the carved portions were burnished. Sometimes the leaf will go black when burnished, in which case it and the bed will need to be rubbed down and the latter stages of the operation repeated.

Matting

In this final operation, designed to mat and press down the gold-leaf, the gilder applies a thin size – known as 'matting size' – from right to left over the whole gilded surface, including any burnished areas that look as if they might be too bright.[15]

Patina

After burnishing and matting the gilder goes over any patches with a stiff brush and a little water to make them easier to patinate (ill. 76).

Patination is necessary to make the patch blend with the rest of the gilded work or, where the gilding has been renewed completely, to reproduce the look of the original gilding. In fact in the latter case patination may be even more necessary, for example where freshly gilded woodwork might produce an unpleasant contrast with faded original upholstery, or a bright new frame clash with an Old Master. The gold can be worn slightly with glass-paper and covered with a glaze to tone it down. Every restorer has his own method, using gouache, spirit varnish or turpentine. The wisest solution, however, is to stay with rabbit-skin glue, a material already basic to the gilding process, and apply a coat of this tinted with water-colour to produce the desired effect.

Once more we come up against the fact that restoration, if it is properly done, is an extremely time-consuming business. Unfortunately some gilders are tempted to take short cuts by using various unor-

76
Renewing patina. A Louis XIV picture frame on which the gilding has been patched. Centre right, the new gold has already been partially patinated. At top left the process is almost complete.

77
Oil gilding a picture frame. The gilder has just lifted the gold-leaf with his tip from the 'cush' held in his left hand and is laying it with his right hand.

78
Georges Jacob, walnut canapé, Paris, 1785 (0.98 by 1.81 by 0.60 m), restored in 1968. Jacob's invoice details the work he did: the canapé was given 'several coats of white gilding ground', then 'all the ornaments were rubbed down and smoothed with water'; he went on to trim 'carefully', paint 'two coats, to wit: backgrounds in pale lilac and the said ornaments set off in white lead', and finally he sized and varnished 'with a good fine varnish'.[19] The original paintwork had faded badly. The light ground (two or three coats) was discreetly trimmed, the carving being already very delicate; the paintwork was then largely restored on the basis of preserved material.

thodox methods such as applying ground and bed with a spray gun and using electric dryers, which are not as good as natural drying.

OIL GILDING
Already in use in seventeenth-century England,[16] this process reached France in the eighteenth century and was analysed by Watin in his book (ill. 77).

The wood can be prepared in two ways: either with a mixture of yellow or red ochre powder and an oil varnish or with a gesso ground similar to that used for water gilding but covered with a coat of shellac varnish. Sometimes a bed is laid on top. The gilder then applies his mordant, a reboiled oil preparation that can be bought ready-made.[17] This must be applied sparingly with a hard brush and as much as possible of it removed afterwards, because if it is too thick it will not dry properly and the gold will blacken when laid on top. Depending on its composition, this mordant will require three, six or twelve hours to dry. The gold-leaf is then laid directly on to it, allowed to dry, and finally covered with matting size or a clear shellac and spirit varnish.[18] It is then patinated.

Oil gilding is much quicker than water gilding, but it becomes dull and it cannot stand much handling.

Gold size is a quicker-drying mordant that needs only half or three-quarters of an hour. It is used for patching oil gilding.

SILVERING

Silvering – much used in Italy, for example – is done in the same way as gilding, using either the water or the oil process. Silver-leaf is thicker than gold-leaf. To prevent it from oxidizing it is covered with clear varnish (or gold varnish, if the intention is to imitate gilding).

Paintwork

The restoration of painted furniture involves, when the paintwork is applied to a ground, very similar problems to that of gilded furniture; the same remarks apply as regards the techniques involved, and the solutions used are parallel (ill. 78).

If the restorer is dealing with a glue-based paint that has flaked, he removes everything that no longer holds, renews the ground, trims it where it was trimmed originally, and retouches with a glue paint (or gouache) diluted with rabbit-skin glue – a process that is closest to traditional painting.

If the piece needs repainting completely, the restorer uses the same method as for gilding to cover the wood with several coats of ground, filling any holes with putty. He then rubs down and if necessary trims. The actual painting is done with a mixture of whiting and rabbit-skin glue tinted with pigments and powder colours. Certain pigments alter with age, and stable colours should be chosen. Occasionally, since glue paint is sufficient to cover up blemishes in the wood, it is applied directly without a ground. In either case two coats of paint are generally required.

Having retouched or completely renewed the paintwork, as the case may be, the restorer must now fix it with an invisible protective coating. There are various possibilities: spirit varnish gives paint a glossier look but darkens it slightly; a mat finish can be achieved with natural wax or a glue scumble, both of which are transparent, though wax fixes less effectively than varnish.

Oil-paint can also be applied to a ground and likewise calls for two coats. More resistant than glue paint, it needs no protection, though it may take on a patina.

In the case of furniture where a gilded decor in relief is set off by a painted background, ground is laid uniformly over the whole piece and the restorer renews the gilding first, in order to avoid having laying water run over the paintwork; he then repaints the background with glue or oil-paint, whichever was used originally.

110

AUXILIARY TECHNIQUES

There are few materials that furniture manufacturers have not made use of at one time or another, and it is not often that one can restore a piece of furniture without finding oneself working on materials other than wood. Sometimes the restorer has to rely on the assistance of craftsmen from other fields, although it is preferable that he should himself take care at least of leather work,[1] bronze mounts and locks; furniture sent out for these jobs always risks getting dirty or damaged. Again, the main thing to remember in connection with these auxiliary techniques is that when restoring a piece of antique furniture one should always retain a maximum of old components and be careful that one does not leave the upholstery and accessories looking too new for the wood.

Upholstery

As Roubo wrote, 'It is very necessary that the Joiner should have some knowledge [...] of the Art of the Upholsterer [...] lest he do anything that may interfere with the latter's work; but that on the contrary he makes it easier of execution, that both may strive in harmony for the perfection of the whole.'[2] One of the things that restorers often have to do for upholsterers is to glue blocks in the four corners of seat frames to take the upholstery nails. Fixing these blocks is a particularly delicate business, and upholsterers frequently complain of their being too high or too low; it is their height that determines that of the upholstery and governs the appearance of the piece.

The memoranda of furniture dealers in the past show the importance of upholstery on seats and beds. The original upholstery, however, was often replaced very early on – and has been many times since. This has of course tended to damage and alter the character of much antique furniture. Eighteenth-century chairs were later fitted with sprung upholstery, which was virtually obligatory from the Restoration (1814) onward but to which they were structurally unsuited. Chairs designed to take a cane seat were subsequently upholstered in cloth. Where a piece has been lucky enough to retain its original upholstery or at least an antique replacement, the restorer must carefully preserve not only the material but possibly also the nails – often mercury-gilded – and the webbing, which he will replace in such a way that it shows underneath the seat while his own reinforcement webbing is hidden. Where on the other hand a piece has modern upholstery and one can imagine what it originally looked like, one tries to get as close as possible to that original appearance.[3]

Upholsterers too are having difficulties with their supplies. The quality of webbing is deteriorating (it used to be made of hemp but is now jute) and so is that of animal horsehair (superior to vegetable horsehair). This is why used animal horsehair, for example, is always salvaged and recombed.

Bronze mounts

Gilded or varnished bronze mounts can also present problems. Their history will invariably have been a stormy one. They too were often changed very early on (see p. 12); they may have broken, or the gilding may have been worn off with cleaning; others will have disappeared altogether for a variety of reasons and may or may not have been replaced. Some restorers like to forget all this history and make a clean sweep, fitting a complete set of mounts corresponding to the period of the piece. One only has the right, however, to reproduce missing elements from identical surviving elements, particularly where it is a question of functional mounts such as handles, castor sockets and keyhole plates. Furthermore, even this may be difficult to accomplish in view of the very limited number of workshops now doing lost-wax casting (sand casting often lacking sufficient precision) and mercury gilding, and in any case both processes are very expensive. Sometimes one makes do for economy's sake with electro-gilding or gilding with nitrate of mercury. The right colour can be obtained by heating the mount if it is gilded or – which is more difficult – by tinting the varnish if it is varnished. Let me repeat that it is better to leave a piece with ill-assorted mounts that will deceive no one than to risk compounding one's predecessors' errors.

SOLDERING

When a broken mount needs to be soldered, two methods are possible. Soft soldering (with tin) has the advantage of not impairing gilded work, but it is best confined to mounts that are not going to be exposed to any rough stuff afterwards. It is not very strong and in fact needs a strengthening piece fixed to the back of the mount. It also takes a long time to scratch off the tin if one wants subsequently to replace it by a hard-soldered join. Hard soldering (with copper) is stronger but has the grave disadvantage that it cannot be done on gilding; consequently it involves stripping a fairly large area on both fragments to be joined. The metal is heated red-hot and the restorer melts on to the fracture either flakes of copper, which give an invisible join after the gilding or varnish has been restored but which are unfortunately no longer obtainable, or copper in rod form, which has now replaced the flake and gives a less solid join on which varnish and gilding do not take very well. A hard-soldered joint will consequently need chasing before it is regilded or varnished.

The bronze mounts running round pieces of furniture are often riddled with screw-holes. These are filled with bronze pins that are then brazed, the restorer taking care not to damage the surrounding bronze as he files them down.

CLEANING

Mounts are never cleaned on the piece of furniture but are always taken off first, otherwise the moisture that gets into the screw-holes will tend to work its way out again and corrode the gilding and on the other hand rust the screw threads, causing them to break when unscrewed. Whatever product and method – dipping, brushing – are used, it is essential to rinse well afterwards and dry the mount in deal sawdust, which penetrates into every crevice. Proprietary detergents should be avoided. Gilded bronze is best cleaned with soapy water, to which some restorers add a little alkali,[4] or with a decoction of quillaia bark[5] with a little fermented beer in it, both preparations being used warm and applied with a nylon brush. Varnished bronze can also be cleaned with soapy water. If revarnishing is necessary, the bronze is stripped, polished and degreased; it is then heated with a blowlamp for a few seconds to turn it yellow and immediately brushed with shellac varnish. Crude bronze can also be treated with cellulose varnish; it is heated afterwards to obtain the required shade. The only upkeep that bronze mounts require is dusting with a soft cloth.

Marble

Marbles were often waxed. If necessary they can be cleaned with turpentine and refinished with beeswax.[6]

CARE AND MAINTENANCE

To prevent a restored piece of antique furniture from deteriorating further, the first necessity is that it should be kept in a constant atmosphere or one that changes only very gradually. The relative humidity should be about 50% and the temperature between 15° and 20°C, the ideal being 18°C and anything higher than 20° being detrimental to furniture as indeed it is to its owner's health. Once the climatic conditions for which the piece was designed have been recreated, the materials of which it is made up – wood and glue – will retain their properties and their adhesion. Particularly to be avoided are any abrupt changes, to which veneered furniture is even more sensitive than solid-wood furniture. All furniture is at its most sensitive in spring, when extra vigilance is called for. Never place a piece of furniture in front of a heat source or a window or in a draught. The atmosphere should be humidified all the year round, even in summer, by means of actual humidifiers or by the more simple method of having a few vases of flowers or potted plants in the room. Another very good method is to use a saturated sponge in a plastic container, placing it under the piece of furniture or even inside it when, as is often the case, there is an empty space, e.g. alongside the drawers of a commode; evaporation will produce enough moisture to keep the piece in good condition but not enough to impair the glue.

There are other sensible precautions one can take to preserve the structure and appearance of a piece of furniture. When a piece needs to be moved it should be lifted rather than dragged along the floor, particularly if it has things on it or the drawers or cupboards are full. Marble tops are best removed first and carried on edge rather than flat. Once a piece of furniture is in place it must be steadied, primarily to stop the legs working loose and starting to wobble. Loading should be kept within reasonable limits, and any doors must be kept closed to prevent them from warping. In particular, never leave the front of a secretaire open all the time because it will warp and because heat trapped underneath will damage the marquetry. Where a piece has a lock and key it is best to leave the key in the lock; otherwise a burglar may inflict serious damage. Marble tops must be steadied too and supported where they overhang in case they break when leaned on. Heavy marbles are actually dangerous, and one must be careful that the console or whatever it is does not collapse under the weight. In fact it is a good idea to secure a console by means of a metal bracket fixed to the wall, designed to take the weight either of the back rail of the console or of the marble itself.

Lower down, furniture is even more vulnerable and needs to be protected against feet and brooms. It is also a good idea to protect the bottoms of the legs of certain types of furniture – chairs in particular – with steel 'domes';[1] available in various sizes, these are fitted with one or three spikes that are driven into the bottom of the leg, which the 'dome' then protects without damaging the floor.

Drawers that stick can be rubbed along the bottoms of the sides or along the lower runners with paraffin wax or a dry cake of soap.

Veneered furniture requires special attention. If a piece of veneer starts lifting it can be held in place provisionally with adhesive tape, which if the varnish is sound will not damage it. Flat surfaces of Boulle marquetry table or commode tops – can be covered with a pane of glass to prevent the brass from becoming dislodged.

The colour of a piece of furniture can be preserved by fitting the windows with blinds and by moving the piece about to expose different sides of it.

Finally, as regards upkeep, let us just run through a few of the best-known recommendations. Care should be taken when dusting veneered furniture that the duster does not catch and lift pieces of the veneer. Above all, never clean with linseed-oil (see p. 78) as people used to advocate in the nineteenth century;[2] dust becomes embedded in the oil and eventually forms a crust. And never polish a piece before you have dusted it, because dust is abrasive. An antique waxed piece need only be rubbed with a clean, dry, soft but not fluffy cloth. And it is usual to repolish such a piece once a year, using beeswax rather than a modern silicone product. Where the piece is varnished, wax is unnecessary; in the short term it may bring out the colour, but by trapping the dust it will create a layer of dirt that will need to be stripped if at some later date one decides to re-varnish. Varnished furniture only needs dusting; for more thorough cleaning, a commercial reviver can be used (see p. 78). A word of warning here: varnish dissolves in alcohol so is easily marked by drinks, and it softens when brought into contact with a hot surface. To avoid unwanted build-up on the surface of a piece, one does not wax painted, gilded or lacquered furniture. Painted furniture can be cleaned with a commercial reviver. Gilded furniture only needs dusting. For cleaning lacquer, the author of a recent book on the subject recommends a commercial reviver, or alternatively white rum.[3]

NOTES AND DIAGRAMS

INTRODUCTION

1 French restorers describe such a piece as *blanc bleu*.

2 'Memorandum and account of the repairs and works that I, Juan Miguel Borobey, cabinet-maker to the household of the Queen Mother, carried out for Her Majesty between October and the end of December 1691. Firstly, on 10 October 1691, to cleaning and repairing a tortoise-shell cabinet used as a wash-stand with table and leg of the same material, on which I worked in Her Majesty's bedchamber together with four men until the 27th of the month, applying various pieces of tortoise-shell and ebony mouldings, a goldsmith cleaning the silver and regilding the gilt elements, mounts, and figures with which it was decorated, adding four bronze figures and repairing the table, which was split down the middle, the whole job, materials and labour, amounting to 1500 reals … On 9 December of the same year, to repairing an all-tortoise-shell table decorated with 32 small mirrors inserted in it with children painted on them, replacing several missing mirrors, numerous pieces of tortoise-shell, and nearly all the moulding around, cleaning and plating the leg mounts, the whole job, materials and labour, amounting to 450 reals … To repairing another small table of pear wood, very badly damaged, and fitting blued mounts, the repair amounting to 40 reals.' Madrid, Archivo de Palacio, Sección administrativa, leg. 631 (Ebanistas).
'To Potain, joiner, for repairs made by him to furniture in the apartments of the late Monseigneur le Prince and those of Madame la Princesse', 35 l. 5 s.; 'To Guillemard, cabinet-maker, for repairing a green ebony marquetry wardrobe in the alcove of the Gold Room, providing bellows for the fire and a walnut wardrobe', 87 l. Paris, Archives nationales (Arch. nat.), R³ 296 – Accounts of the estate of the Prince of Condé, 1711, pp. 272, 282.

3 Paris, Arch. nat., Minutier central, étude XXVIII, liasse 64, 8 August 1702.

4 L. Courajod, *Livre-journal de Lazare Duvaux, marchand-bijoutier ordinaire du Roy, 1748–1758*, Paris, 1873, vol. II, pp. 32, 135, 244.

5 He did so as early as 1776 and on several occasions subsequently for the famous bureau supplied in 1769 (P. Verlet, *Le Mobilier royal français,* vol. II, Paris, 1955, pp. 65–75), and in 1777 for the commode supplied for Louis XVI's bedroom at Versailles in 1775 (*ibid.,* vol. I, Paris, 1945, pp. 21–4).

6 Paris, Arch. nat., 0¹ 3524, 'Ordre établi dans le Gardemeuble de la Couronne dès l'année 1666', memorandum of May 1753. See also P. Verlet, *French Royal Furniture*, London, 1963, pp. 46–9.

7   See for example G. de Bellaigue, *The James A. Rothschild Collection at Waddesdon Manor. Furniture, Clocks, and Gilt Bronzes*, London, 1974, vol. I, p. 182.

8   A. Setterwall, 'Some Louis XVI furniture decorated with *pietre dure* reliefs', in *Burlington Magazine*, vol. CI (1959), pp. 425–35.

9   On an Italian bureau (G. de Bellaigue, *op. cit.*, vol. II, pp. 574–6) a pair of English drop-front secretaires (sale in London, Sotheby's, 5 October 1973, p. 70, no. 116).

10 In Paris, round about the year 1808, the cabinet-maker Jacob-Desmalter said he had twelve workmen 'employed every day on various maintenance jobs in houses we service regularly' (D. Ledoux-Lebard, *Les ébénistes parisiens du XIXᵉ siècle (1795–1870), leurs œuvres et leurs marques*, Paris, 1965, p. 251).

11 *Ibid.*, pp. 76, 516.

12 *Ibid.*, p. 473.

13 A. Sauzay, *Musée impérial du Louvre, Musée de la Renaissance, Série B. Notice des bois sculptés ...*, Paris, 1864, pp. 37–8.

14 F. Williamson, *Les Meubles d'art du Mobilier national*, Paris, n.d. [1888

15 D. Ledoux-Lebard, *op. cit.*, p. 290.

16 G. de Bellaigue, 'Edward Holmes Baldock, II', in *Connoisseur*, no. CXC (September-December 1975), pp. 20–1.

17 P. Eudel, *Le Truquage. Altérations, Fraudes, et Contrefaçons dévoilées*, Paris, n.d. [1908], p. 297.

18 For many, restoration is a one-man job. A furniture restorer working on his own restores between twelve and twenty pieces a year.

19 E.g. to a lacquer bureau supplied to Louis XV in 1744, which in 1787 was altered and veneered in 'yellow wood' (P. Verlet, *Le Mobilier royal français*, vol. I, pp. 8–11).

20 L. Courajod, *op. cit.*, vol. II, pp. 50, 289.

21 D. Ledoux-Lebard, *op. cit.*, p. 442.

22 L. Courajod, *op. cit.*, vol. II, pp. 276, 349.

23 The historian is always delighted to find such information because of its interest as regards the history and origin of the piece. See G. de Bellaigue, *The James A. Rothschild Collection ...*, nos. 49, 65, 67, 86, 87, 94, 116, 117. On one of Riesener's bureaux preserved at Versailles a nineteenth-century restorer left a notice warning his successors about the thinness of the veneer (P. Raymond, *La Marqueterie*, Dourdan, 1977, pp. 24–5).

MATERIALS AND TOOLS

1   The suggestion has been made in France that the state could help certain trades by promoting the setting-up of stockpiles of products that are hard to come by. See P. Dehaye, *Rapport à Monsieur le Président de la République sur les difficultés des métiers d'art*, Paris, 1976, pp. 91–2.

2   Roubo, *L'Art du Menuisier*, vol. III, book III, *L'Art du Menuisier-Ebéniste*, Paris, 1774, pl. 278.

3   2.25 mm at most (Roubo, *op. cit.*, p. 799). I am indebted to Messrs. Douville, pit sawyers of Villeneuve-la-Garenne (Hauts-de-Seine), for assistance and information. See also P. Ramond, *op. cit.*, pp. 40–2.

4   Roubo was already complaining of this back in the eighteenth century: 'Cabinet-makers have always been wont to make the very greatest

secret of the composition of their dyes in order to retain exclusive possession of them [...]: so it is that the majority of the compositions used by the old cabinet-makers have either not come down to us or have been poorly imitated; and that those in use at present are either defective or, if they are good, cannot be improved, since those whose property they are refuse to disclose how they are made' (Roubo, *op. cit.*, p. 792).

TYPES OF DAMAGE

1   A wood is referred to as 'fined-grained' when the pores are not visible on the surface (as in fruit-tree woods, for example).
2   Roubo, *op. cit.*, vol. III, book II, 'L'Art du Menuisier en Meubles', Paris, 1772, p. 601; see also *idem*, book III, pp. 811–12, 866–7.
3   L.-S. Mercier, *Tableau de Paris*, vol. IX, Amsterdam, 1788, p. 245.
4   Ph. Burty, 'Le Mobilier moderne', in *Gazette des Beaux-Arts*, XXIV (January-June 1868), p. 43.
5   Furniture deteriorates rapidly as a result of negligence. Of 24 lyre-backed mahogany chairs delivered to the Princesse de Lamballe at Versailles in 1787, by 1791 there were '4 backs broken and half a lyre missing ... plus 1 front leg of one of the said chairs broken' (P. Verlet, *Le Mobilier royal français*, vol. II, pp. 150–1).
6   Mme de Girardin, *Le Chapeau d'un horloger*, Paris, 1855, p. 3.
7   In France, the Centre Technique du Bois and the Centre Technique Forestier Tropical publish a list of selected products: *Produits de préservation du bois homologués à la marque de qualité CTBF. Liste des produits et guide de l'utilisateur, 1er janvier 1977*, Paris, 1977.

8   This needs to be done carefully; if the hole is blocked with wood dust, the injected material may squirt out into the restorer's eyes, with dangerous results.
9   E.g. 'Paraloid B 72', an acrylic resin that dissolves in xylene or toluene. This is a fairly dangerous product and must not be inhaled.

WOODWORK

1   For the different sorts of gilding and painting, see the chapter GILDING AND PAINTWORK.
2   If it is glue-based it is much more difficult to remove. Spirit is used.
3   So much so that identification marks may disappear.
4   See, for example, E. Klatt, *Die Konstruktion alter Möbel*, new ed., Julius Hoffmann, Stuttgart, 1973 (text in German, English and French), which discusses the construction of many pieces of European furniture.
5   Wood is said to be cut with the grain when its fibres lie in the direction of its length.
6   Standard equipment in the cabinet-maker's workshop.
7   It is best to select old beech; the tacks may split beech that is too fresh.

VENEER

1   Roubo, *op. cit.*, vol. III, book III, pl. 290, 299, 303.
2   Inlaid marquetry on a Louis XVI piece may have been added later as enrichment.
3   Where the panel has a regular curve another practical method is to mould a sheet of cardboard by pressing it against the curve and then mount the cardboard on a wooden support; the

unglued veneer, fixed to the card, will retain its shape.

4 In France the Centre Technique du Bois (10, avenue de Saint-Mandé, 75012 Paris) among other bodies undertakes the identification of types of wood.

5 See also P. Ramond, *op. cit.*, pp. 58–65.

6 The Paris firm of Buffard used to supply strings already made up, either simple or composite, but it stopped trading in 1973.

7 Roubo, *op. cit.*, vol. III, book III, p. 863.

8 One of the most reliable ways, though of course it calls for quiet surroundings.

9 Irons are best heated on a gas stove, where their temperature can be controlled. Several irons are heated at once and used in succession as soon as they are warm. There are also electric veneering irons.

FINISHING VARNISHED AND WAXED FURNITURE

1 A scraper is a flat, rectangular piece of steel. It is held in both hands, and the edges of the two long sides do the scraping. These may be straight, bevelled or curved to fit concave surfaces. It is a particularly difficult tool to sharpen.

2 Above 20°C certain precautions have to be taken. In summer, for example, bottles of varnish are kept in cold water, otherwise the varnish sticks.

3 The best type of pad is made of knitted wool. It is a good idea to have a number of pads, some of them used only for filling and others only for varnishing. Rather than keep them in tins, which they tend to rust, it is best to place them in glass jars sealed hermetically to stop them drying out.

4 In hot weather the restorer will soak his pads a bit more because the spirit will evaporate faster.

5 Especially filling pumice, which could turn the varnish white.

6 So the spirit should be a little warm to make it evaporate faster and stop it forming a sludge on contact with the pumice. A small quantity of wood dust kept after rubbing down may be added to the pumice.

7 Watin, *L'Art du Peintre, Doreur, Vernisseur*, 2nd ed., Paris, 1773, p. 276.

8 Roubo, *op. cit.*, vol. III, book III, pp. 862–5.

BOULLE MARQUETRY

1 See Roubo, *op. cit.*, p. 983.

2 'Cabinet-makers do not use bare tortoise-shell, that is to say that they do not apply it to the wood direct; but after shaping it and reducing it to thickness, they line it in order to provide a backing and prevent the glue and the markings of the groundwork from showing through. This lining consists simply of a coat of black or red painted on the flesh side of the shell and afterwards covered with a piece of paper glued on top of it [...]. These two colours are the only ones given to tortoise-shell, at least in the ordinary way, and red is the one most in use currently' (*Idem*, p. 1011).

3 *Idem*, pp. 983, 995, and 1001.

4 D. Ledoux-Lebard, *op. cit.*

5 L. Courajod, *op. cit.*, vol. II, pp. 247, 277.

6 Christie's sale catalogue, London, 30 November 1972, p. 22, no. 70.

7 Paris, Arch. nat., 0¹ 3631, memorandum by Riesener, 2nd semester 1784; 0¹ 3635, memorandum by Riesener, 2nd semester 1785.

8 D. Ledoux-Lebard, *op. cit.*, pp. 359, 82.

9 According to Roubo, tortoise-shell in his day varied in thickness between three-quarters of a *ligne* (1.7 mm) and one and a half *lignes* (3.4 mm); see Roubo, *op. cit.*, p. 1008.

10 In the Louvre restoration workshop this putty is made up as follows: powdered tortoise-shell, collected at the sawing and rubbing-down stages; limewood sawdust to absorb the adhesive well; vinyl adhesive; powder colour or gouache, depending on the colour of the tortoise-shell (e.g. Bismark brown, raw sienna, burnt sienna, burnt umber); and a little lithopone to harden the mixture.

11 Roubo, *op. cit.*, p. 1020.

12 P. Ramond, *op. cit.*, p. 56.

GILDING AND PAINTWORK

1 Woodworm will not penetrate the ground but may form galleries beneath it.

2 P. Verlet, *Le Mobilier royal français*, vol. I, pp. 75–91.

3 H. de Balzac, *Le Cousin Pons*, 1847. Where a piece of furniture has been regilded recently in France, the inside surfaces – e.g. the insides of console surrounds or seat rails – are often painted yellow (a darker shade than the ochre size covering the ground).

4 This is apparently what Watin refers to as 'Greek gilding'; see Watin, *op. cit.*, pp. 163–5.

5 E.g. the folding chairs from Marie-Antoinette's *salon des jeux* at Compiègne when they were transferred to Napoleon's chambers at Fontainebleau in 1806; see P. Verlet, *op. cit.*, p. 86.

6 Watin, *op. cit.*, pp. 180–1.

7 In France there is still one firm manufacturing rabbit-skin glue. It needs to be soaked overnight before use. It is then melted down in water in the ratio of 100 g of glue to a litre of water. The solution must be neither too weak nor too strong. It goes off quickly and is best kept in a refrigerator or at least in a cool place, and in summer the restorer will make up less in advance than in winter.

8 This fill is prepared as follows. A quantity of whiting is placed in a pot and a 'funnel' made in the middle of it into which the liquid glue is poured (this must not be too hot). The ingredients are then stirred from the funnel outwards, care being taken not to form any lumps. The putty, which must remain sticky, is kneaded with warm hands to soften it. It is then wrapped in a damp sheet or placed in an earthenware jar and covered with a damp cloth. It does not keep for long and should be used the same day or resoftened the next day.

9 This is a kind of reed that grows in ponds and is becoming rather difficult to get hold of nowadays because no one collects it any more. The stems are cut to remove the knots and the pieces soaked to make them swell and become supple. They are used wet and gathered into a bundle. The ends that are in contact with the surface to be smoothed can be cut off at an angle.

10 A note by Chatard, a gilder employed by the Crown Furniture Repository under Louis XVI, well illustrates the importance of trimming. He invoiced for regilding the screen from Marie-Antoinette's bedroom at Versailles as follows: sizing and ground (18 *livres*), trimming (120 l.),

ochre sizing and bed (18 l.), gilding (112 l., plus 36 l. for gold), burnishing (24 l.); see P. Verlet, *op. cit.*, p. 91.

11 Gilders were already using this material. Gilding can in fact be done with pipe clay by mixing it with glue to make a kind of milk that when applied to the wood forms a very light ground without filling in the carved work. The process saves time because this type of ground smooths itself and does not need rubbing down. Afterwards the restorer can proceed by either the water process or the oil process. The Germans manufacture a vinyl bed that should not be used for restoration purposes, particularly because when patching it is impossible to match the original bed.

12 The various stages of gold-beating can be summarized as follows. An ingot of pure gold is rolled into a thin strip that is then cut up into small pieces. These are mixed with the metals (usually silver and copper) needed to produce the alloy that will give the required colour, and the whole lot is melted down in a crucible. The alloy is then cast into an ingot, and the ingot is rolled out to produce a strip of metal of about the thickness of a postcard. This is cut into small squares of 5 by 5 cm or slightly larger. Each of these is gradually flattened, at first by three or four machine beatings in a roughing mill. The squares, piled in packs, are separated from one another by a sheet of parchment during the initial beatings and subsequently by a very thin film of plastic. Such a stack is referred to by gold-beaters as a 'pack'. After two or three initial beatings the pack is separated and the leaves of gold cut into quarters and piled into a fresh pack. After its final mechanical beating the pack is beaten by hand with a hammer weighing approximately 6 kg. French gold-beaters work sitting down, their German colleagues standing. Finally the pack is separated again and the gold-leaf extracted with tweezers and arranged in 'books'. See C. Ruegsegger, 'L'or battu', in the *Revue des douanes* (Swiss), 1975, no. 2. I am grateful to M. Didier Charrier, gold-beater at Sens, for information on this matter.

13 Watin, *op. cit.,* p. 148.

14 The brushes employed by gilders (ill. 73) used to be manufactured by craftsmen brush-makers but are now produced industrially and are of inferior quality. Similarly gilder's tips are now thicker than they were; one used to be able to see through them.

15 Some of the operations Watin refers to — applying special grounds for gilding with green or lemon gold, applying a so-called 'vermilion' solution after burnishing and matting — are apparently no longer performed by present-day gilders.

16 See also R. Edwards, 'A set of carved and gilt furniture at Knole and its restoration', in *The Connoisseur*, vol. CXLV (March-June 1960), pp. 164–8.

17 The mordant currently produced by one French firm consists of linseed-oil that has been heated to between 250° and 280°C with raw umber and a dash of litharge.

18 But certainly not a turpentine varnish, which would remove the mordant.

19 H. Lefuel, *Georges Jacob, ébéniste du XVIIIe siècle*, Paris, 1923, pp. 278–82.

AUXILIARY TECHNIQUES

1 Leather for desk tops is glued in the same way as veneer, glue being applied to both the carcase and the back of the leather and expelled by rolling from the centre outwards.

2 Roubo, *op. cit.*, vol. III, book II, pp. 609–10. The upholsterer for his part has to wrap the legs of chairs to protect them as he does his job.

3 Using documentary sources such as *Les Styles dans le décor intérieur. Les sièges de style de Louis XIII au Second Empire*, Paris, Fédération Nationale des Selliers et des Tapissiers de France, 1970 (illustrated with slides).

4 But alkali must never be used on a mount still in position because it attacks varnish.

5 Also called 'soap bark', this has the property of forming a lather.

6 When a marble needs replacing (see ill. 50) the restorer is advised to consult M.G. de Bellaigue's catalogue, *The James A. de Rothschild Collection...*, which reproduces the moulding profiles of nearly all the marbles on the furniture in that collection.

CARE AND MAINTENANCE

1 There are rubber ones too, but they are not adequate for this purpose.

2 See for example Nosban and Maigne, *Nouveau manuel complet de l'ébéniste et du tabletier*, Paris, 1887, p. 383 (Manuels-Roret).

3 A. Lorac-Gerbaud, *L'Art du laque*, Paris, 1973, p. 94.

DIAGRAMS

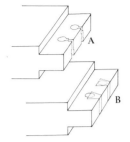

Figure 1
A. A damaged tenon.
B. Repaired with dovetails.

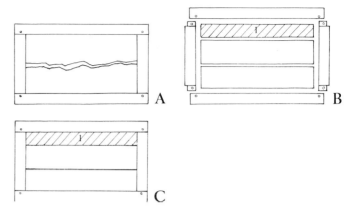

Figure 3   Repairing a split panel with a making-out piece.
A. The split panel.
B. After dismantling. The edges of the split have been straightened and the making-out piece (1) prepared.
C. The reassembled panel with the making-out piece in position.

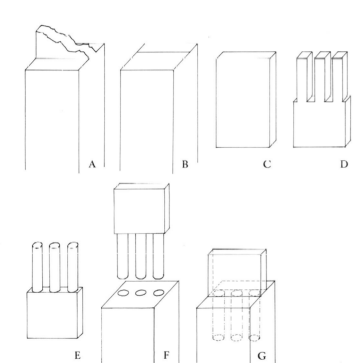

Figure 2   Replacing a broken tenon with a rounded comb tenon.
A. The broken tenon.
B. The root of the broken tenon has been flushed off.
C. The piece of wood from which the comb tenon is to be cut.
D. and E. Making the comb tenon.
F. and G. Fitting the comb tenon.

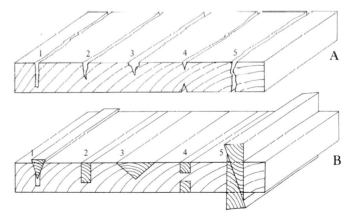

Figure 4   Repairing a split panel with in-fills.
A. The split panel.
B. 1 This in-fill is no good; it does not fill the split.
  2–5 Different types of in-fill to fit splits 2–5 in figure 4 A.

123

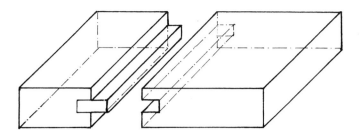

Figure 5   False tongue.

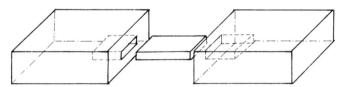

Figure 6   False tenon.

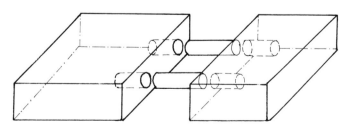

Figure 7   Pins.

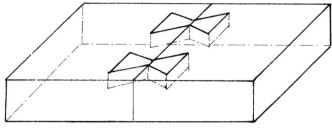

Figure 8   Double dovetail keys.

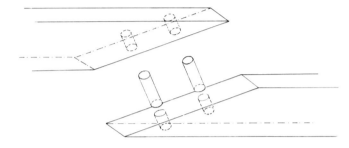

Figure 9   Scarf joint with two pins.

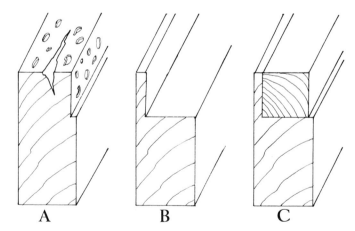

Figure 10   Repairing a seat rail with a false rebate.
A. The split seat rail.
B. After chiselling out.
C. Fitting the false rebate.

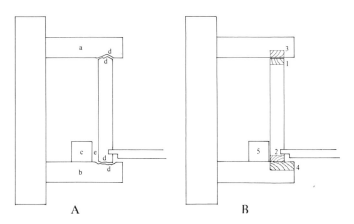

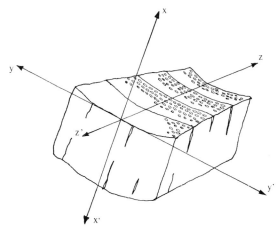

Figure 11 Overhauling the runners on the left-hand side of a drawer.

A. Before the repair.
   a) upper runner
   b) lower runner
   c) drawer guide
   d) worn parts
   e) play between drawer and drawer guide

B. After. Four thicknesses have been glued on: on top of (1) and underneath (2) the side of the drawer, in a groove in the upper runner (3), and in a rebate in the lower runner (4). The drawer guide (5) has been unglued and reglued alongside the drawer.

Figure 13
The different directions in a piece of wood (after A. Villière, 'Le ‹jeu› du bois et les moyens pour le réduire', offprinted from the *Courrier de l'Industriel du Bois et de l'Ameublement*, 1973, no. 2, p. 4).

x x'   axial (along the grain)
y y'   tangential
z z'   radial

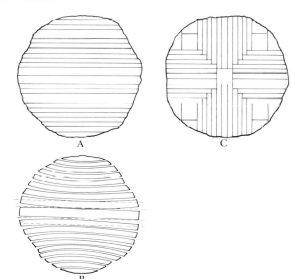

Figure 14
A.   Log cut tangentially (slab-cut).
B.   Effect of drying on slab-cut boards.
C.   Log cut on the quarter.

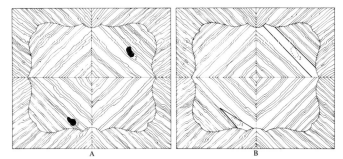

Figure 12 Patching
A. Diamond-pattern veneer with two holes in it (1 and 2).
B. Outline of the matching patches (1 and 2).

BIBLIOGRAPHY

1. Wood; General

CAMPREDON, J., *Le Bois*, Paris, P.U.F., 5th ed., 1975 (Que sais-je?, no. 382).

HOURS, M., 'Etat des recherches en matière de conservation des biens culturels en bois', in: *Musées et collections publiques de France*, no. 129 (1st quarter, 1975), pp. 7–11.

KÜHN, H., *Erhaltung und Pflege von Kunstwerken und Antiquitäten*, vol. I, Munich, 1974.

MONCRIEFF, A., 'Review of Recent Literature on Wood (January 1960 – April 1968)', in: *Studies in Conservation*, vol. 13 (1968), pp. 186–212.

PLENDERLEITH, H. J. and WERNER, A.E.A., *The Conservation of Antiquities and Works of Art. Treatment, Repair and Restoration*, London, 1971.

Les Colles dans l'industrie du bois, Paris, Cahiers du Centre Technique du Bois, series III, no. 97 (n.d.).

Les Ennemis des bois dans la construction et l'ameublement, Paris, Cahiers du Centre Technique du Bois, series I, no. 31 (June 1958).

1970 New York Conference on Conservation of Stone and Wooden Objects, 2nd ed., International Institute for Conservation, London, 1971, vol. II.

2. Craftsmanship

CHANSON, L., *Traité d'ébénisterie*, 7th ed., Dourdan, n.d.

RAMOND, P., *La Marqueterie*, Dourdan, 1977.

ROUBO, *L'Art du Menuisier*, vol. III, book II, *L'Art du Menuisier en Meubles*, and book III, *L'Art du Menuisier Ebéniste*, Paris, 1772–74 (reprinted Paris, 1977).

WATIN, *L'Art du Peintre, Doreur, Vernisseur*, 2nd ed., Paris, 1773 (reprinted Paris, 1975).

3. Restoration

RODD, J., *The Repair and Restoration of Furniture*, London, 1954.

VERLET, P., *Les Meubles français du XVIIIe siècle*, Paris, 1956 (2 vols., L'Œil du Connaisseur).

WENN, L., *Restoring Antique Furniture*, London, 1974.

ACKNOWLEDGEMENTS

The author wishes to express his keen appreciation of the assistance generously given by the following: the restorers who have kindly shared with him their professional experience, in particular MM. René MIRAMOND and Claude PENOT, restorers at the Musée du Louvre, and Jacques PENOT;

MM. Jean Alot, Jean-Michel André, Claude Collot, Roger Delaunay, Henri Desgrippes, Vincenzo Fancelli, Michel Germond, Maxime Goujon, Pierre Klieski, Henri Lefeuvre, Lucien and Christian Leprince, Germain Mathel, Paul Mériguet, Mlle Anna Østrup, MM. Victor von Reventlow, François Servas;

M. Jean Taralon, General Inspector of Historical Monuments, Director of the Laboratoire de recherche des Monuments historiques;

M. Marcel Stefanaggi, head of the laboratory, and M. Bernard Callède, of the Laboratoire de recherche des Monuments historiques;

Mme Lola Faillant, head of the documentation service in the Laboratoire de recherche des Musées de France;

Dr. Franz Windisch-Graetz, Director of the Österreichisches Museum für angewandte Kunst, Vienna; the Conservators of the Musée Camondo, the Musée national du Château de Malmaison, and of the Musée Bossuet at Meaux, and the President of the Syndicat d'initiative at Tonnerre, who kindly authorized reproduction of works from their collections;

M. Alain Moatti;

M. Edmond Tanner, head of the cabinet-making workshop at the Musée du Louvre;

Mme Marie-Françoise Leca, Mlle Marie-Laure de Reviers, and Mme Florence Faidherbe;

and his friends and colleagues Ségolène Bergeon, Danielle Gaborit-Chopin, Daniel Meyer, Jean-Pierre and Colombe Samoyault.

INDEX

Acetone, 67
Acid, 35, 70, 71, 78
Alcamer, 24
Alkali, 70, 98, 113
Ammonia, 67
Araldite, 25

Baldock, E. H., 8
Balzac, H. de, 94
Blocks, 43–6
Boulle, A.-C., 81
Boulle marquetry, 50, 54, 81–92; finishing, 90, 92; levelling off, 89, 90; regluing, 90; ungluing, 84–8
Brass, 84, 85, 88, 89
Bronze, 81, 94, 112, 113
Burty, Ph., 28

Cassel extract, 70
Carving, 13, 25, 48
Charcoal, 77, 78
Cleaning, 7, 97, 113, 115
Copper, 81, 86, 88, 112

Dasson, H., 80
Delorme, A., 84
Disinfection, 31–2
Dowels, 36, 38, 40, 42

England, English, 25, 103, 104, 109
Epoxy adhesive, 25
Eudel, P., 9

Filling, 37, 38, 74, 75
Flexan, S., 7
Formol, 32, 104

Gamma radiation, 32, 33
Gas impregnation, 32
Germany, German, 8, 81, 104
Gilding, 13, 34, 35, 84; bronze, 94, 112, 113; electro-, 112; oil 109, 110; water, 93, 94, 96, 97
Glass-paper, 68, 74, 78, 90, 92, 101, 102, 106
Glue, 21, 23, 32, 35, 52, 54, 65, 70, 90, 94, 101, 105; animal, 21, 23, 97, 98, 106, 110; fish, 23, 24. See Epoxy, Vinyl
Gluing, 28, 31, 36, 38, 39, 40, 42, 44, 48, 49, 55, 57, 60, 76, 86, 89; scarf, 47
Gold-beating, 94; gold-leaf, 94, 98, 102, 104, 106, 110. See Gilding
Grenoble, Nuclear Research Centre, 33

Incised work, 13, 58, 68, 92
Inlaid work, 42, 50, 57
Insects, 28, 30–3, 66, 78
Iron, 37, 54, 57, 61; hot iron method, 23, 38, 54, 60
Italy, Italian, 21, 49, 103, 104, 110
Ivory, 81

Lacquer work, 8
Ledoux-Lebard, D., 81
Levasseur, E., 84
Louis XIV, 7, 82, 101
Louis XV, 7, 50, 80, 81, 94, 101

Louis XVI, 81, 101
Louis XVIII, 8
Louis-Philippe, 8, 84

Marble, 113, 114
Marie-Antoinette, 94
Mercier, L.-S., 28
Meudon, 103
Montigny, P. C., 84

Paintwork, 34, 35, 110, 115
Paris, 7, 20, 31, 80, 82, 93, 103
Pewter, 81, 84, 88, 92
Polishing, 76, 77, 78; French, 74, 75, 78
Potassium, 35, 67, 71

Rémond, F., 8
Riesener, J.-H., 7, 82, 84
Roubo, A. J., 20, 28, 50, 58, 80, 88, 111
Rubbing down, 12, 67, 68, 69, 78

Séverin, N.-P., 82, 84
Shellac, 58–60, 92
Silvering, 110
Sormani, L., 80
Spirit, 67, 70, 71, 76, 78, 94, 98, 105, 106
Staining, 67, 69, 70, 71
Stripping, 67, 78; chemical, 34; dry, 34, 67; gilding, 34, 97; hot-water, 34, 35; paintwork, 34; potassium, 35
Switzerland, Swiss, 25

Tarsia certosina, 49, 66
Tenons, 38, 40
Tortoise-shell, 49, 81, 84, 85, 86, 88, 89, 90, 92
Tripoli, 77, 78

Upholstery, 12, 30, 33, 37, 48, 111, 112

Varnishing, 71, 72, 75, 76, 78, 110, 113, 115, cherry shellac, 75; polyester, 75; revival of, 78; shellac, 75, 110; white, 75
Veneer, veneering, 20, 21, 23, 30, 34, 37, 39, 40, 49–66, 68, 69, 76, 79, 87, 115; caul, 61, 62, 64, 65; frames, 64; hammer, 60, 61; iron, 23; sand, 63; saw-cut, 20, 21, 57; strap, 65
Verlet, P., 7
Vinyl adhesive, 24, 25, 33, 37, 47, 87, 89

Watin, 80, 93, 97, 104
Wax, waxing, 32, 33, 35, 37, 66, 69, 71, 74, 84, 92; beeswax, 74, 80, 113, 115; filling, 67, 68; lost-wax casting, 112; polishing, 67, 71, 72, 80
Weisweiler, A., 84
Whiting, 32, 37, 100, 110
Wood: beech, 19, 28, 30, 40, 70; burr, 21; chestnut, 70; deal, 81, 113; ebony, 21, 50; hornbeam, 21; king-wood, 21, 70; mahogany, 21, 30, 38, 54, 71, 75, 79; maple, 21; oak, 28, 40, 42, 70, 71; pear, 21; plane, 21; rosewood, 21, 54, 69, 70, 75; sap-wood, 30; snake-wood, 21; sycamore, 21; violet wood, 21, 54, 58, 75; walnut, 30, 70, 101

Photo credits

The photographs reproduced in this volume were taken by M. Maurice Chuzeville (1, 2, 7–10, 13–22, 24–29, 30–32, 34, 36–38, 39, 41–44, 46–48, 51–64, 68, 71, 74); M. Georges Routhier (49, 65–67, 69, 70, 72, 73, 75–78); M. Jacques Penot (23, 33, 45); M. Claude Penot (5, 35, 40); M. Yves Grossot (12); La Réunion des Musées nationaux (3); Le Musée du Château de Fontainebleau (4); Österreichisches Museum für angewandte Kunst (6); Le Conservatoire national des Arts et Métiers (11); Le Musée de Meaux (50). Diagrams by Klutt Mouchet, Gérard Pichelin, Claude Penot and René Miramond.

Printed in August 1977 by Imprimerie Hertig + Co. S.A., Bienne. Photolithographs: Kreienbühl + Co. S.A., Lucerne. Binding: Burkhardt, S.A., Zurich. Layout and production: Ronald Sautebin.

Printed in Switzerland